CONCISE DICTIONARY OF METAPHORS AND SIMILES

A Perfect Reference for Students of all age groups. Useful guide for aspirants of IAS, CAT, GMAT, Civil Services, IELTS, TOEFL & Other Examinations

V&S PUBLISHERS

Published by

F-2/16, Ansari Road, Daryaganj, New Delhi-110002
☎ 011-23240026, 011-23240027 • *Fax* 011-23240028
Email info@vspublishers.com • *Website* www.vspublishers.com

Regional Office Hyderabad
5-1-707/1, Brij Bhawan (Beside Central Bank of India Lane)
Bank Street, Koti, Hyderabad - 500 095
☎ 040-24737290
E-mail vspublishershyd@gmail.com

Branch Office Mumbai
☎ 022-22098268
E-mail vspublishersmum@gmail.com

Follow us on   

For any assistance sms **VSPUB** to **56161**

All books available at **www.vspublishers.com**

ISBN 978-93-505715-2-1
Edition 2014

Printed at Param Offseters Okhla New Delhi-110020

Publisher's Note

simile is where two things are directly compared because they share a ommon feature. The word *as* or *like* is used to compare the two words. For xample, *as* cold *as* a dog's nose. The clouds were *as* fluffy *as* cotton wool. he clouds were fluffy like cotton wool. A simile is only one of dozens of ecific types of metaphor. In short, a simile is a type of metaphor in which e comparison is made with the use of the word *like or its equivalent*: My ve is like a red, red rose.

Considering the growing importance of English in all spheres of life, e recently published an EXC-EL Series (Excellence in English Language) mposed of four books - English Vocabulary Made Easy, English Gram-ar & Usage, Spoken English, and Improve Your Vocabulary. We thought e have done our bit. No sooner, the Series hit the market; a volley of read-s sought our help to improve diction, presentation and attractiveness of eir conversation – both in writing and speaking.

Being aware that our existence as a publishing house depends solely on fulfilling readers' expectations and continued patronage, we decided come out with something that can add spark to any conversation while aking it appear interesting. This Dictionary of Metaphors & Similes is the tcome. There are three more companion dictionaries on – Idioms, Phrases d Proverbs..

This book explains the meaning behind hundreds of Metaphors & Sim-s that you hear or read in English each day. *The meanings are shown in italics*. In order to keep it concise, this dictionary attempts to present mos commonly used Metaphors & Similes. Having an exhaustive one will jus overwhelm you with thousands of Metaphors & Similes that nobody uses anymore. English remains immensely popular, attractive, articulate and rich language but the confusion between Metaphors & Similes is sometimes 'tough nuts to crack'.

What led us to publish this? Metaphors & Similes appear in every language, and English has thousands of them. They are often confusing In order to understand a language, you must know the precise meaning of metaphor and simile in that language mean. Unless you know the underly ing difference between the two, you will get completely befuddled.

We would be happy to have your views and comments for improving the content and quality of the edition.

METAPHORS

Introduction

What are Metaphors?

A metaphor is a figure of speech that describes a subject by assertin that it is, on some point of comparison, the same as another otherwis unrelated object. Metaphor is a type of analogy and is closely related t other rhetorical figures of speech that achieve their effects via associatio comparison or resemblance including allegory, hyperbole, and simile.

In simpler terms, a metaphor compares two objects or things witho using the words "like" or "as". One of the most prominent examples of metaphor in English literature is the All the world's a stage monologue fro As You Like It:

Following is a list of Metaphors with their Meanings. Rea understand and learn them as they may be of great help in your day to da conversations and in making sentences as well as in writing good Englis

800 lb gorilla
A powerful organization that runs without paying heed to rules and laws.

A battle
Referring to something that may be very difficult.

A beacon for fellow workers
A point of attraction for others.

A burnt child dreads the fire
Experience brings caution.

A classroom
Somewhere where one learns, and corrects one's mistakes.

A cleanskin
A person without a criminal record or other blemish on that person's reputation

A david and goliath battle
A struggle between two parties who are not evenly matched.

A game
Any situation which involves rules; life.

A gem is not polished without rubbing
People only improve through life's hard experiences.

A Herculean cleaning of the stables
A thorough revision of operating procedure

A kick in the shins
An unexpected and undeserved setback

(To be a) Moose
Refers to an athletic man.

A Roland for an Oliver
Tit for tat.

A stab in the dark
A sheer guess

A stiff upper lip
Obstinate courage in the face of pain or adversioty

A stitch in time saves nine
Timely repairs are the least costly

A tale out of fruit-cake land
An account or explanation so unreal as to be more credible in a fairy-tale.

A tidal wave of (something)
An overwhelming manifestation of some emotion or phenomenon; an overwhelming manifestation of some emotion or phenomenon.

Abandon ship
To abrogate one's responsibilities or abandon a project.

Above one's head
Beyond one's comprehension.

(To be) Abrasive
Rough/ hurtful.

Add fuel to fire
To make a bad situation worse

(To be) Adrift
Wandering.

(To be an) Airhead
To be dull in thinking, to be a fool or a stupid person.

(An) Albatross
An emotional burden.

All fired up
Fully prepared.

All he touches turns to gold!
Refers to a successful trader. (After the story of Midas whose thoughtless request that whatever he touched should turn to gold was granted by Dionysus.)

All hell broke loose
Great confusion.

All systems go
To be ready to proceed as fast as possible.

All-embracing
To be comprehensive.

Am whacked!
Exhausted.

America is a melting pot
Culturally diverse.

An Aladdin's cave
A place full of unexpected wealth Storehouse, accumulation of material or artistic wealth.

An ass in a lion's skin
A hectoring coward.

An epic
An account of heroic acts.

An iron anvil should have a hammer of feathers
Subdue the harsh with patience and gentleness.

An old flame
An old lover.

An urchin
Someone who creates trouble.

Angel
To be very good-natured.

Appeal from philip drunk to philip sober
Wait to return to normality.

Apple of my eye
To be the most adored person to someone.

Apple-polishing
Trying to win somebody's favour by flattering or giving gifts.

(To be) Arcadian
Rural and simple.

Argus-eyed
Watching jealously.

Asleep at the switch
Inattentive.
Assembly-line justice
Rough justice.
At a loose end
Not knowing what to do.
At crossroads
A decision making situation.
At first blush
At the beginning.
At first hand
Personally.
At full throttle
Using all your efforts, energies.
At white heat
Of intense passion.
Aunt Sally
Used when referring to a target for criticism.
Authority is a chair, it needs legs to stand up
Authority requires the support of people.
Away with the fairies
Out of touch with reality, often of sufferers from senile dementia.

B

Back to the drawing board!
Jocular expression used when the failure of a plan or contraption can be attributed to some earlier oversight or miscalculation.

Bad bobbin
To be the worst.

(To be) Bait
Lure; to make someone angry.

Ball the jack
Work fast; gamble and risk everything on one try.

Bang/knock their heads together
Bring sense by means of mutual confrontation.

Barn-burner
Destroyer.

Be a heckle to
Be an annoyance to.

Be a recipe for (disaster/happiness/success etc)
If something is a recipe for disaster, happiness, success etc., it is very likely to cause this.

Be all thumbs
Fumbling and awkward.

Be born/come on the wrong side of the blanket
Be bastard-born.

Be in disharmony
Refers to quarrelling.

Be on the right rail
Think or act correctly.

Be run down
In poor condition, out of health, low; uncared for, decaying, lacking maintenance—of property and machinery.

Be two folk
Be unfriendly.

Be wound up
Under tension, ready for action, excited.

Bear the palm
Be a victor.

Bear's service
Trying to help, but actually doing more harm than good.

Bed of nails
Painful experience.

Bed of roses
Something that is very pleasant and easy.

Before the ink is dry
Immediately.
Beg like a cripple at a cross/on a bridge
With great importunity.
Beggars can't be choosers
To one who in asking a favour is too particular.
Begin/lead the dance
Take the lead in any course of action.
Being cold as ice
Very severe.
Belling the cat
To try to perform a difficult task.
Bend the bow of Ulysses
To take inspiration from a great man.
Better to wear out than rust out
Better to be active than stagnate.
Between Bel's two fires
In great difficulties.
Between hammer and anvil
Between two equally devastating evils.
(Am) Bewitched
Fascinated, as if under a spell—especially of a man by a woman.
Big red button
For the purpose of starting something.
Big wheel
An important person.
Billy has found a pin
A sarcastic disparagement.
Binding
To be compulsory.
Bird of ill omen
A person with a reputation of bringing bad luck.
Bird's-eye maple
Light-skinned attractive black woman
Birth-control hours
Shift or night work that results in one spouse sleeping by day and the other at night.
Bite the file
Intentionally injure yourself; consciously seek a painful experience.
Bitter truth
Harsh truth.
Bittersweet memories
Good and bad memories.
Black magic
Evil magic.
(To be) Black
To be impure, evil.
Black-hearted
To be wicked.
Blacksmith's daughter
Padlock or key to a door or gate.
Blizzard of activity
Seemingly active movement.
Blot on the landscape
An intruder or intrusion that spoils otherwise pleasing surroundings.
Blot out
Annihilate.
Blow a gasket/fuse
Lose temper, lose control.

Blow hot and cold
To go back and forth.
Blow hot and cold
To vacillate.
Blow your boiler
Lose your temper.
Blow/let off steam
Release surplus energy, suppressed emotions etc.
Blowed in the glass
Genuine .
Blown away
To be surprised; taken away by excitement.
Blue as wad Long
Standing but irregular practice, especially in industry.
Blue in the face
To be upset.
Blue skies
Signify happiness.
Bluebeard
Husband of many successive wives.
Bluebeard's key
The symbol of opposite reaction.
Boil not the pap before the child is born
Don't do work earlier than it is required.
Boil
To get very angry or upset; to swell.
Boiling frog
Reference to people who can't seem to react to gradually occurring changes.
Boiling mad
Very angry.
Boiling landscape
A group of solids, over time, acting as a liquid. Time is an essential factor in the states of matter.
Bolt from the blue
An unexpected shock
Bond
To join, bond, fasten; to guarantee.
Bookworm
A person who likes to read a lot.
Borrowed plumes
Second-hand knowledge or opinions which someone displays as their own.
Bosom friend
Refers to wad of money concealed in bra.
Bottom feeder
A person who lives a very lowly life, barely surviving.
Bottom out
Reach the lowest or worst point before an upturn.
Bound to
Fated to do something.
Brain-child
The creation of one person's thought, ideas.
Brass ring
Living life to the fullest.
Bread and circuses
Satisfaction of shallow desires of the population at the expense of good policy.

Break a flint upon a feather bed
To use means ill-matched to the task.
Break his horn-book
To subject oneself to displeasure.
Break the mould
To make further repetition impossible.
Break the sound-barrier
Break wind.
Break the thread
Interrupt the continuity—of a story, dream etc.
Break
To end something.
Breaking news.
To break is to end consistency, thus become new. Break = change.
Breathing fire
Filled with anger, inside and out.
Bright mind
Intelligent, smart.
Brilliant idea
A really good idea.
Broken heart
Your heart is not literally broken into pieces; you just feel hurt and sad.
Brought the pack to the pins
Dwindled away the goods.
Brought up to speed
Prepared for entry into a gang.
Brownie points
Recognize someone's achievement.
Bubbly personality
To be full of energy, very high-spirited, always energetic.
Bubbly personality
Enthusiastic, cheerful personality
Bucket brigade
A method of moving items by passing those items from one person to another, in a chain.
Bucking for a raise
To buck is to attempt to force change.
Buffer state
Country situated between two possible enemy states.
Bugbear
Needless fear.
Buridan's ass
A victim of indecision.
Burn-out
Physical, artistic or professional exhaustion through over-activity
Burst his boiler
Come or bring to grief.
Burst
To be full of/filled with something.
Bursting with flavor
Taste is territorial, and strong flavor is an escapee. Our senses occupy space.
Bury your head in the sand
Shrink from facing the facts.
Butt-shut
Be consistent.
By one and one spindles are made
Don't expect to do everything at once.

C

Cadmean victory
A victory which is also filled with loss.

Caged emotions
Feeling boxed in, full of hatred

Camel's nose
Permitting small changes which will later lead to unpredictable and negative changes.

Carry the seeds of change
Carry the potential for change

Carry weight of the world
To appear or behave as if burdened by all the problems in the whole world

Carry weight
To be influential

Case-harden
Make hard, callous.

Cassandra
a woman who forecasts danger.

Cast in mould
Created in that character.

Cast in someone's mould
Mto take after another person

Casten in a calm
Neat.

Cast-iron
Irrefutable, unbreakable.

Cat's paw
Another's tool.

Cease the day
To make avail of all opportunities that are provided in life.

Chapter of accidents
Refers to a series of unforeseen events.

Character assassination
Defaming a person's character.

Chase the rainbow
Pursue an ideal, illusion. (From the saying that a crock of gold lies buried at the rainbow's end.)

Cheek by jowl
To be associated closely; close to each other

Chicken out of
Abandon

Chill out!
A slang asking someone to calm down.

Chilly
Unsociable.

Chimerical
Imaginary; fantasy.

Chinese puzzle
A perplexing enigma.

Chink in someone's armour
A weakness in someone's defences that creates an opportunity to do something that otherwise could not be done.

Chink of light
A small hope of a solution or breakthrough.

Chip in
To contribute financially.

Circuit-breaker
An event that breaks the tension in a dispute.

Clam up
To refuse to talk.

Clamp down on
Suppress, restrict firmly.

Clean sweep
A complete clearing out.

Clean up a mess
To sort out mistakes or neglect.

Clean up one;s act
To fix up the deficiencies in one's affairs.

Clear skies
Devoid of danger.

Clear-cut
Sharply defined, unmistakable.

Clip someone's wings
A reduce another rperson's freedom to act as that person thinks fit.

Closed book
To be secretive.

Coarse (about or with something/one)
Rude, crass.

Cock and bull story
An improbable tale.

Cockatrice egg
Starting point of deadly danger.

Cog in the machine
A mere worker without personal identity.

Cold feet
To be nervous.

Cold fish
To be an unemotional person.

Collide
To clash, collide, hit etc.

Colorful remark
A joyous and multi-faceted remark.

Come alive to
Become aware of.

Come apart at the seams
To break down.

Come back to haunt someone
To be a constant reminder to a person.

Come clean
To confess.

Come down on someone like a hammer
With crushing speed and finality.

Come down with a thud
To be suddenly disillusioned.

Come home
Be born.
Come out into the open
To start being frank.
Come out of the closet
To admit publicly one's homosexuality.
Come past the smithy
Acquire a sharp temper.
Come through loud and clear
To be well understood.
Come to life
Fully realised.
Come unstuck/unglued
Miscarry; deteriorate into chaos; fail.
Conjecture
Forecast.
Consumed by love
Filled with love.
Cool
A slang to indicate that something is fashionable in many aspects.
Copper-bottom
A driver who works long hours.
Copper-hearted
Untrustworthy.
Core-dump on
Complain, explain fully to, pour one's heart out to.
Couch potato
A very lazy person.
Countdown has started
Death is fast approaching
Court disaster
To do something that will be harmful to onself.
Crab-apple
To be harsh in speech and behaviour.
Crank up
Excite, make eager, get started.
Crazy/silly as a two-bob watch
Completely mad.
Crocodile tears
Fake crying.
Crocodiles' teeth are white daggers
Comparison of crocodile teeth to sharp knives- their teeth are very sharp and inflict pain.
Cross one's mind
To occur to one's mind, to think of something
Crucible period
A time when radical change takes place.
Cry for the moon
Demand the impossible, the unattainable.
Cry out for
Demand vehemently, imperiously, pitifully; require urgently.

Cry wolf
Forfeit your own credibility by false alarms.
Cuckoo
To be crazy.
Cuff ears
Police order.
Cultural mosaic
A mix of different cultures, ethnicities etc.
Cut blocks with a razor
Waste talents.
Cut down to size
Deflate a pompous person; reduce them to a proper level of importance.
Cut off at the web's end
Finished before time.
Cut your teeth
Reach an age of discretion.
Cute as a wooden box
When used sarcastically, the wooden box is thought of as a coffin

D

Dance attendance
Wait obsequiously, assiduously on another.

Dance barnaby
Move quickly or unevenly; make haste.

Dance to someone else's pipe/tune/whistle
Follow someone else's desire or lead.

Dance/march to a different tune
Change policy, activity, allegiance

Daniel come to judgement
To be the perfect example of wisdom.

Darby and Joan
Devoted old couple.

Dark horse
A person with unsuspected talents.

Dead duck
To have failed, or to be in a hopeless situation.

Dead in the water
Hopeless case.

Dead tired
To be extremely tired.

Deaf as a nail
Hard/right [straight]/sure as nails.

Deep dark secret
A secret which cannot be revealed under any circumstances.

Deep despair
Lot of sadness.

Deep, dark thoughts
Secret thoughts.

Diamond in the rough
A person who is good natured but may lack respect for the law and social etiquette.

Did he fall or was he pushed?
An ironic enquiry suggesting that things might not be as innocent as they seem.

Dim view
A very narrow viewpoint.

Dinosaur
Someone who is very old.

Dip one's pen in gall
To write with bitterness.

Dipped in the Shannon
Not in the least bashful.

(To be a) Dodo
A fool.
Doesn't know yet he's been born
Has no experience of life in the world.
Dog in the manger
A type of selfishness where someone prevents another having what he needs, although he does not want it himself.
Dog one's trail
To follow.
Dog-eared pages
Pages that have been constantly folded over a long time.
Dog-tired
To be very tired.
Don't fall before you're pushed
Don't anticipate trouble.
Don't let your imagination run away with you
One should not mix fantasy with reality.
Don't lift me till I fall
I do not need your help yet; don't interrupt, I have not finished.
Don't take the axe out of the carpenter's hand
Don't deprive folk of the wherewithal.
Done and dusted
Completely finished.
Don't bite off more than you can chew
One should not try to achieve more than one is capable of achieving.
Dot the i's
Go into detail.
Down on all fours
Depressed, in recession.
Down the line
Through to the end, to a logical conclusion.
Drag one's feet
Delay deliberately.
Draw a picture
Explain simply and clearly
Draw the king's/queen's picture
Forge coins.
Drive it home
Ensure full understanding.
Drive not a second nail until the first be clinched
Finish one job before starting another.
Drive the nail home/to the head
Push a matter to a conclusion.
Drive the nail where it will go
Only attempt that which is possible.
Driving force
Compelling agency; person, ideal impelling to action.
Drop into the lap of
Be acquired without effort
Drop/dump/throw in the lap of
Delegate a problem to; shift the burden to.
Drop/throw off the mask
Reveal yourself in your true character.

Dry spell
Shortage of something.

Dry straight
Turn out all right in the end; survive a testing time.

Dry-nurse
Instruct seniors in the requirements of their rank or position; one appointed to do so.

Duck-hover
Manipulator; someone who uses unfair business practices.

Dying to
Very excited/anxious to.

E

Earn his/her wings as
Acquit him/herself creditably as.
Easy targets over which trainee
Aircraftsmen practise their bombing runs.
Eat dog for another
Oblige.
Eat well of the cresses
Be sure to remember.
Eat-the-pack
Spendthrift.
Education is a gateway to success
Education brings about success.
Electrify
To Startle.
Elephant in the room
Referring to something which is obvious and presented directly but is still ignored.
Eleven cuts to the hank
Mentally lacking.
Embark
To begin.
Enchant
Captivate by beauty or wonder; put in a state of magical euphoria.
End of story! Really, that is all there is to be said about it.
Usually pronounced with an air of finality subsequent upon information that needs no further explanation.
End on a sour note
Ending something badly.
Endowed with
To be gifted naturally.
End-product
Final form
Espouse/embrace
To adopt something and work for it; dedicate oneself to something.
Even steaming!
Said when one matches the effort of the other.
Every jewel needs a setting
A beautiful woman, unpartnered, is wasted.

Every pedlar must carry his own pack
There are some things you can only do for yourself.

Every pedlar praises his own pack
Self-advertisement is no recommendation.

Every schoolboy knows that!
Telling someone about their lack of simple knowledge.

(To) Exist
To be.

Eyes peeled
To watch very carefully for something Life is a dream Life is short and goes by so quickly, it seems like a dream.

F

Face like a bagful of spanners
Rough and lumpy.

Face like a smacked arse!
Feeling sorry for oneself.

Face like a smith's anvil
Hard and unyielding.

Face like a welder's bench
Disagreeable.

Face of brass/brassy/brazen
Impudently bold.

Face the music
Face somebody's reprimand.

Fade off to sleep
You don't actually fade, you simply go to sleep.

Fail to see (your) logic
I don't understand your viewpoint.

Fairy godfather
Sponsor, backer generally.

Fairy godmother
Anonymous or unexpected benefactress.

Fairy story
An account or excuse, fanciful but harmless, recognised and denounced as implausible.

Fall flat on your face
Come to sudden and unexpected grief, fail utterly.

Fall to the ground
Fail through lack of support; be abandoned.

Fast as a rivet
Securely fixed.

(To) Father
Be the originator of, produce generally; own responsibility for.

Feed into
Insert for processing.

Feeling blue
Feeling sad.

Feeling rough
Not feeling well.

Fell the web
Finish off.

Find a false prophet
Be disappointed by someone.

Find a horse-nest
Laugh without reason.

Find a mare's nest
Make a fancied or trifling discovery that you imagine to be important.

Fine-drawn
Exaggerated.

Finish Aladdin's window
Try to complete a work started, but left unfinished, by a greater genius.

Fire is day, when it goes out it's night
Fire brightens the surroundings, when it is put out, only darkness is left.

Fishing for something
Expression which is used to signify that the person is looking for something that is difficult to obtain.

Fits to a T
Exact.

Flash-point
Political temperature at which war or a crisis arises; the event that triggers a crisis.

Flaxen Pale
Golden, blond—usually of hair

Flirt with an idea
To give something little amount of consideration, but no serious attention.

Flogging a dead horse
Wasting time on something even though its fate has already been decided.

Fly on the wheel
One who claims credit for what he has not done.

Fly-by-night
Unreliable, because likely to disappear overnight.

Fly-by-sky
Flighty, imaginative, volatile, unsteady person.

(To) Foil
Someone or something juxtaposed so as to improve, by contrast, another's appearance.

For want of a nail
Attention to detail is important.

Force of a steam hammer
Irresistibly crushing.

Force someone's hand
To take action causing another person to react

Forge
Create something strong and durable.

Fork in the road
Choosing from various choices.

Four Asian Tigers
Referring to the highly developed Asian economies- Singapore, Taiwan, South Korea and Hong Kong.

From the same smithy
Just as bad; congenitally similar.

Frozen with fear
To be very scared so as to be unable to move.

Full blooded
Complete; wholehearted, unadulterated.

G

Gain the upper hand
To attain, after some effort, an advantage over another person.

Galvanise
Rouse by shock into life or action.

Gamut the complete range or scope of something
The whole gamut of human emotion

Gas-bag
Empty but excessive talker

Gather up the threads/pull the threads together
Bring disconnected elements into a coherent whole, or at least an orderly interrelationship.

Geared to
Adjusted, adapted to...; dependent on.

Get a foot/a toe in the door
Gain entry

Get a hair in one's neck
Pay off old scores.

Get a head of steam behind...
Obtain powerful support or driving force.

Get close to the bone
To cause discomfort by being accurate

Get down to brass tacks
Reach the vital part of the work; work in earnest.

Get off the ground
Get properly started, make a beginning of the work.

Get one's lug in the loof
Severely dealt with.

Get one's screw out
Become angry

Get out of one's pram
Become excited, agitated, angry; out of control.

Get round a man's neck-hole
To gain control over him.

Get steam up/get up steam
Prepare to go into action

Get the lease
Understand rightly.

Get the lion's share
Get the largest share.

Get the picture
Have enough information to understand the situation.

Get under feet
Interference

Get weaving
To start.

Get cold feet
to lose courage
Get/take the steel out of...
Get the best out of something or someone.
Giant-killer
An individual who challenges a large organisation.
Gimlet-eyed
Keen-eyed, given to peering into things.
Gipsy's warning
A dangerous warning.
Gipsy-legged
Slender ankles
Give (someone) the cold shoulder
To show that one is unwilling to be friendly with (a person)
Give a handle to...
Give cause for rumour, suspicion etc.
Give a pound of flesh
To pay dues.
Give birth to...
Bring into existence.
Give full marks for
Give credit to someone for their work.
Give her rock another tow
Give her something else to think of.
Give him room to grow
Give him personal space.
Give pap with a hatchet
Do a kind act in an unkind manner; punish someone under the pretence of doing them a kindness.
Give someone the cold shoulder
Ostentaniously to ignore a person
Glowing review
A good review.
Glued to
Closely applied to.
Glued-on
Added haphazardly without being integrated with the main part of the work.
Glued-up
Assembled at random.
Go against the grain
Go contrary to nature.
Go all/flat out
As fast as possible
Go begging
Be available for anyone who wants it.
Go for the doctor
Make an all-out effort.
Go hand in hand
To be inseparable.
Go home and kick the dog
To take out one's anger on someone who is weaker.
Go into a flat spin
Panic, lose control.
Go into orbit
Reach heights beyond belief or control.
Go into rhapsodies
Enthuse extravagantly.

Go into your dance
Begin a prepared speech, act, performance, 'sell' etc.
Go nthrough something with a fine-tooth comb
To conduct an extremely thorough investigation
Go on an overdrive
Over-response.
Go on shirt-buttons
Be very erratic.
Go over his mother's thumb
Break from all control or authority.
Go pear-shaped
Go wrong, amiss.
Go round by Robin Hood's barn
Go indirectly.
Go the whole hog
Do something without reservation and completely.
Go through the flint-mill
Endure problems; suffer badly.
Go with your finger in your mouth
Without food or money.
Go/run off the rails/track
Abandon your usual routine; become demented; turn criminal; have an extramarital affair.
Gobsmacked
Surprised and astounded.
Going on like Sokespitch's can
Proceeding excellently.
Grate on
Annoy.
Grease in the fist
Bribe.
Grease/oil the wheels
Make things go smoothly.
Great engines turn on a little pin
An unimportant person may have an important function in a large organisation.
Great weights hang on thin wires
Important decisions may be taken on slender evidence; unimportant persons may be the instruments of great events.
Greek gift
One which is bound to lead to destruction.
Green light
Signifies that it is safe to move ahead.
(To be) Green
To be new or inelegant or immature.
(A) Greenie
A novice.
Grey area
Neither this nor that in a situation.
Grey skies
Referring to bad times.
(To) Grill
To question.
Grind to a halt
Stop slowly but inevitably.
Grit in the oil
An obstruction, obstacle to smooth working.
Gun with no bullets
Something incomplete and therefore useless for the desired purpose.

Hag knots
Tangles in horses' manes, made by witches for stirrups.

Hag ridden harassed
Oppressed in mind (as if ridden by a witch in a nightmare).

Hag's teeth
Protruding lumps of matting.

Hail of bullets
Hard and driven

Hair by hair you will pull out the horse's tail
Slow and sure succeeds best.

Halting speech
Stammering or hesitant speech.

Ham
Someone who shows off.

Hammer and pincers/pinsons
The noise of a horse's hind-shoes striking the fore shoes.

Hammer into the floor like a tack
Punish.

Hammer it out
Solve problem by hard application

(To) Hammer
Force into.

Hammer-and-tongs/-pinsons
Using full effort and all resources.

Hand over fist
Rapidly overtaking each other during progress towards a common goa

Handle to his name
A title.

Handpick someone
To choose a person carefully for that person's individual attributes

Handy as a gimlet
Quick, smart, useful.

Hang by a thread
Maintain a precarious connection.

Hang together (in/on a string)
Cohere, be consistent—of argument; be united,

Hang upon the skirts of
Keep close to someone, not venture far from them.

Hanging over one's head
Refers to An imminent misfortune.

Hard-bitten
Toughened by experience

Hard-boiled
Toughened by experience

Hard-wired
Of inherent skills and talents that emerge with maturation rather than being initiated by specific teaching.
Harmony
Referring to good understanding.
(To) Harness
To control; to join.
Has a chip on his shoulder
Is annoyed about something.
Has a screw loose
His mind is not working properly
Has cut his eye/wisdom teeth/has all his back teeth
Has acquired some worldly experience.
Has his head screwed on right
Is shrewd and practical, has common-sense.
Has his mother's milk in the nose
Behaves like a baby.
Has the gliding angle of a brick
Of an aircraft with poor gliding performance.
Have a bad/good nail in oneself
being naturally bad/good.
Have a ball
Have fun.
Have a blacksmith's eye
Be very competent in seeing and judging.
Have a chip on one's shoulder
Unreasonably to resent something
Have a close shave
To have a very narrow escape
Have a green thumb
To be skilled at growing plants.
Have a heart of stone
To be unkind.
Have a needle into
Bear a grudge, spite against.
Have a purple heart
To be brave.
Have a rag on every bush
Court many women.
Have a rod in pickle
Be prepared.
Have a ball.
Have a good time
Have at your finger-tips
Be in complete control; be fully competent.
Have brass/cast-iron balls
To be foolhardy.
Have many/other irons/heats in the fire
Keep other possibilities in reserve.
Have no weft in oneself
To have no energy.
Have one hand tied behind one's back
To work with a handicap
Have other tow to tease
Other things to do.
Have over a barrel
To compromise someone.
Have sour grapes
To be envious.

Have taken one's gears in
To stop doing anything.
Have taken one's reed and gears in
To die.
Have the oil-bottle in your pocket
Be double-faced.
Have the primrose path
To have an easy life.
Have woven one's piece
To reach the end of one's life.
Have butter fingers
A name playfully applied to someone who fails to catch a ball or lets something slip from their fingers.
Having (other) tow on one's distaff
Hard times coming.
Having great taste
To have good choices.
He has a heart
Referring to the intellectual and moral core of humans.
He has ink in his pen
Sexually vigorous.
He has no ink in his pen
Brainless.
He is yellow
Meaning that he is a coward.
Head of tow
With very fair hair
Heart-of-oak
A stable, reliable character; sterling quality.
Heated debate
A very active and vigorous discussion.
Heckle her tow
Scold severely.
Herculean task
Extremely difficult task
Hermetically sealed
Sealed so as to be airtight; closed off from the outside environment
Hew to the line
Adhere to your principles.
Hide one's light under a bushel
To keep others in ignorance of one's sills and expertise.
Hiding behind (a woman's) skirts
Allow a woman to protect you.
Hit the (right) nail on the head
Do or say exactly what is needed.
Hit the buffers
Run out of momentum, cease to make progress.
Hold a winning hand
To be in an unbeatable position
Hold soemone's hand
To give detailed on-the-job- training and supervision
Hold the baby
Be left with an unwelcome responsibility.
Home (in) on...
Direct attention to, concentrate on.
Homespun
Unrefined, but workable.
Hooked to
To be greatly attached or addicted to something/one.
Hug the shore
To be unadventurous.

I

I am charmed by her
I am attracted to her.

I am Engineering a
To Contrive.

I'll give thee bell-tinker
To give one a good thrashing.

I'm talking to the engineer, not the oily rag
In dismissing an interruption.

Icy stare
A very stern stare.

Ideas are water
Ideas are similar to water in the way that both flow, are reusable, are of different forms, are powerful etc.

I'm all thumbs
Very awkward and clumsy, especially with one's hands.

In a cold sweat
To be afraid.

In a groove
In a settled routine.

In a holding pattern
In temporary abeyance.

In a hole
In trouble, inextricably; in financial trouble.

In cold blood
Deliberately and unemotionally.

In full blast
In full operation.

In high gear
In the most active, impressive phase.

In his buttons
Destined.

In its infancy
At an early stage; with much growth still to come. Referring to projects, institutions etc.

In long clothes
In early stages, in 'infancy'.

In more strife than a pork chop in a synagogue
In an embarrassing situation.

In orbit
Escaped from what was previously holding you down or back; elated, exultant.

In the black
To be relieved of financial danger.
In the doghouse
To be in someone's bad books.
In the heat of
Under compulsion of.
In the lap of luxury
Living in supreme luxury.
In the loop
Well-informed, privy to all necessary information.
In the melting-pot
In the process of being changed.
In the red
To face financial problems.
In the throes of
In the hard process of producing something.
In the wrong box
Mistaken.
Infinite spectrum of possibilities
Many possibilities.
Inflamed one's temper
Get maddeningly angry
Ink into
Emphasise and set permanently.
Intermesh with
Be closely involved with.
Iron will
A strong, inflexible determination.
Iron-bound coast
Coast of granite, or rocks dangerous to ships.
It augurs well for
Is a good indication of.
It is as broad as long/as long as broad
There is no difference whichever way you regard it.
It is Greek to me
Not understandable.
It ought to be scrapped!
Should be discarded as obsolete.
It rains by planets
It rains irregularly and unpredictably.
It's been a long, bumpy road
A difficult and strenuous journey
It's like beating a dead horse
It's useless
It's raining men
Abundance of male suitors

J

Judge not a book by its cover
Do not judge someone/thing by face value.

Judgment of Solomon
Using wisdom to bring about justice.

Jump into bed with someone
To enter into a joint enterprise with another person

Jumping for joy
To be very happy.

Jumping the shark
Trying to revive something when it is declining/dying.

Jump-start
Reactivate a stagnant economy, falling production etc. with an outside impulse

K

Keep in leading-strings
Keep a close control over
Keep in the background
Avoid notice.
Keep someone in the dark
Deliberately keep a person uninformed.
Keep the band in the nick
Keep things running smoothly
Keep the oyster
Retain the best part.
Keep the wheel in the nick
Keep on good terms.
Keep your boiler clear!
Look after your (especially abdominal) health.
Kick in the pants
To subject someone to severe criticism.
Kick off
To start some action
Kick one in Slaidburn and they all limp in Newton
Of any inbred district—mutate nomine.
Kick someone around
To abuse a person.
Kick the bucket
Die.
Kick the bucket
Died.
Kick the cat
To take out one's anger on some innocent party
Kick the tires
Make a superficial inspection.
Kill oneself by laughing
To be grtaetly amused
Kill the goose that lays the golden eggs
Foolishly cut off the source of wealth, income, benefits etc.; sacrifice future advantage to the greed of the moment.
King-pin
Main person in cast
Kiss and tell
To give out secrets.
Kiss of death
Something intended to be helpful but resulting in total destruction
Kiss the child for the nurse's sake
Have ulterior motives.

Kiss the dust

To be killed.

Kiss the ground

To revere or bless the alnd, or to be overthrouwn.

Kiss the rod

To accept punishment meekly

Knap the rust

Merely start a job; take offence and leave.

Knock on other doors

Try other openings, alternatives; widen the field.

Knock/rub the corners off

Remove awkward individualities, make more sociable.

Knock/rub the corners off

Remove awkward individualities, make more sociable.

Knock/sing at a deaf man's door

Waste your efforts in making the request.

Knock/throw for a loop

Unnerve, unsettle, throw off course.

Know all the answers

To outwit others.

Kow-tow to...

Admit and submit to an authority.

L

Labour of Hercules
Tasks that require a lot of physical strength.

Labour of Sisyphus/Sisyphean labour
Unending toil.

Lady-killer
Seducer of many women.

Lame duck
A person who has lost.

landslide victory
A huge victory for just one side.

Large as life/life-size
Bigger, more real than expected.

Larger than life
Exaggerated; more than normal

Laugh in a sea of sadness
An optimistic person among many pessimistic persons.

Laundry list
A large set of demands

Lay down guide-lines
Instruct on the policy, principles to be followed.

Lay down the law
To be officious

Lay it on the line
To flatter, eulogise, make a comment in an excessive manner

Lay one's card on the table
To be utterly frank and open, or to honest;y disclose one's position.

Lay/spread it on thick/with a trowel
Overstate, exaggerate, flatter excessively.

Lay it on the line
Put reputation, career etc. deliberately at risk.

Lead one a (pretty) dance
Exact irksome obedience, usually from an admirer.

Lead someone up the gardebn path
Mislead a person by deliberately fallacious arguments

Leading question
A question phrased in such a way as to suggest the answer

Leaf out
To be slightly retarded.

Leap at the halfloaf
Be content with an inferior position.

Leap in the dark

A decisive move into the unknown

Leaping with laughter

Laughing a lot.

Leave no stone unturned

Make a thorough search; try every means to achieve your object.

Leave others for dead

To be vastly superior.

Leave someone clold

To fail to impress

Left in the basket

Neglected.

Lend a hand

To assist.

Let sleeping dogs lie

To let something (a situation) be as it is.

Let the want come at the web's end

Wait to repair a deficiency until the very last moment.

Lick into shape

Train to a useful or presentable standard

Lie at the door of

Become their responsibility.

Lie for/deserve the whetstone

Be an outrageous liar.

Life is a dream

Life is short and goes by so quickly, it seems like a dream.

Life in the fast lane

A very active or possible risky way to live.

Life is a mere dream, a fleeting shadow on a cloudy day

Life is compared to a dream which has to end someday.

Life is a shuttle

Life is never uniform.

Life sucks!:

A way of saying that life is difficult.

Lift the curtain

To Reveal.

Lift the veil of Isis

Go to the core of a great mystery.

Lift your undercarriage

Be off with you! Get going!

Light at the end of the tunnel

A long-awaited improvement in prospect, coming shortly.

Light in a sea of darkness

A ray of hope in a very impossible situation.

Lightening rod

An upcoming achiever.

Lily white

To be pure.

Limp-dick

To be incompetent.

Lint-white

Very white.

Live from hand to mouth

Being in poor financial circumstances.

Live on the smell of an oil-rag

Refuse to spend money on food.

Live wire

To be an enthusiastic, energetic person; lively character.

Load of rubbish
Blatant nonsense.
Lock antlers with someone
To have an argument with another person.
Lock, stock and barrel
Entirely.
Lone wolf
A person who prefers to act without involving others.
Long arm jurisdiction
To be able to pass a judgement on someone who doesn't come under that court's jurisdiction in general situations.
Look after number one
To act selfishly.
Look in the pink
Look well
Look into the crystal ball
See events before they occur.
Look to one's laurels
Remember one's reputation.
Lose one touch
To cease to be familiar withsome-thing/someone
Lose one's nerve
To abandon, out of fear, to do something
Lose one's shirt
Make heavy financial loses
Lose/run out of steam
Lose drive, momentum, urgency, to slow down
Lost one's temper-pin
Become angry.
Love is a camera, full of memories
Like a camera contains the memories of life, love too contains a lot of memories.
Love is a fragile flower opening to the warmth of spring
Feeling of love unfolding to the warmth of a lover.
Love is a growing garland
Love grows with each passing day.
Love is a lemon-either bitter or sweet
Love is like a lemon in the way that it has some bitter facets and some sweet parts.
Love is a thrill ride
Love is thrilling.
Love is in the air
Love is all around.
Love stinks!
love is the worst feeling.

M

Mad-hatter
To be eccentric.
Make (someone) sit up
Compel to be more alert.
Make (something) stick
Make an accusation that can be proven home.
Make a mental note of...
Remember something that has to be said later.
Make a wheelwright of...
Seduce
Make causey webs
To neglect work and roam around idly.
Make mountains out of molehill
To treat a minor problem as though it were a major disaster
Make one's mark
Become memorable.
Make the grade
Surmount a difficulty, pass the necessary standard, work well enough to be accepted, do well enough to go forward.
Make the sparks fly
Cause a lively reaction.
Make whim-whams for a goose's bridle
Waste time on a ludicrous
Making a pig of oneself
Demeaning oneself
Man cannot spin and reel at the same time
Cannot do two jobs at once.
Man in the moon
Remote figure.
Man of iron
Strict character.
Man of one book
To be a specialist in a specific field.
Marry
To join two things.
Mecca
One's goal.
Medusa's head
Something that shocks or surprises a person.
Melt-down
Ultimate disaster; collapse of economy, government etc.
Mesh with
Work together with...; fit in with.

Miles apart
To have grate philosophical differences
Milk for babies
Doctrine, literature etc. simplified for the young or ignorant.
Miss on one/four/all cylinder(s)
Work badly, be in bad condition.
Misty, water-coloured memories
Vague memories
Misty
Dim; hazy.
Money begets money
Will increase, if there is enough to start with.
Monitor
Keep a watch.
Monkey paw
Handle with uncanny skill and diplomacy.
Monkey see, monkey do
Trying to learn something without understand how it works.
Monster/ogre/witch
To be bad-natured.
More belongs to marriage than four bare legs in a bed
Look beyond face value.
Mother hen
An overprotective person
Mother of the mine
A ferruginous rock.
Mother's milk
An essential, elementary need.
Motherhood stae,ent
A statement so obvious and uncontroversial as not to be worth making
Mould on...
Try to imitate.
Mount the ass
To go bankrupt.
Mountain climb
An uphill struggle; difficult journey.
Mountain of strength
Very strong
(To be an) Mouse
Refers to someone who is timid.
Movable feast
An event not customarily held on to a set date
Movbe on to greener pastures
To move to a better environment
Move down a notch
To accept a lower position
Move heaven and earth
To do everything possible
Move the goal posts
Unfairly to alter the rules after some action has already started
Mudslinging
Insults exchanged between different candidates.
Mutton dressed up as a lamb
Foolishly pretend to be younger
My heart's on fire
To be madly in love
My memory is a little cloudy
I can't remember well.
My thread is spun
My life is over.

N

Nail someone
To fix the blame on a person, to secure

Name to conjure with
A powerful and effective name .

Neither rhyme nor reason
No sense.

Neither side nor selvedge
In debt and difficulties

Nerves of iron/steel
Very steady nerves; great patience and courage.

Net
To catch.

Never darken my door again
Do not ever return

New lease of life
Prospect of a better existence

Nick thc thrcad
Put an end to life.

Nip something in the bud
To stop someactivity in its early stages when stopping ti is still relatively easy

No room at the inn
No available space

No way to run a railroad!
A disastrous way to go about anything

Not a penny the better/worse
By no appreciable or noticeable amount.

Not britched yet
Lacking in experience.

Not fit to hold a candle to
Not to be compared with

Not know one's ABC from a battledore
Illiterate.

Not put a foot wrong
Behave impeccably.

Not to be wortha continental
To have no value

Not to have the foggiest notion
To know nothing at all about the subject

Not to lose any sleep over something
Not to worry about some matter

Nothing to make a song about!
Hardly worth considering.

Nought but what was put in with a spoon
No intellectual vigour.

Nourish a serpent in your bosom

To know a traitor.

Nourish vain hopes, resentful feelings etc.

In the heart Foster and encourage them.

Nurse to life

Cherish solicitously; take pains to care for.

Nurse-tree

One left to protect the young crop

Nuts and bolts

Basic ingredients

O

Off the pin of the wheel/the wire
Wandering from the point.
Off-beam/off the beam
On the wrong track, mistaken.
Oil the wheel that squeaks
Deal with the demanding ones first.
Old man of the sea
Burden only discarded with great difficulty.
On a cold day in hell
Never
On a hiding to nothing
Confronted with a hurtful situation without any hope of escaping from it.
On a learning curve
Trying to master an unfamiliar skill.
On automatic pilot
Able to carry on confidently, undistracted by original thoughts, doubts etc.
On cloud nine
Very happy.
On the afternoon turn now!
Not as fit or healthy as before.
On the beam
On the right course, relevant.
On the blink
On the point or in the process of going wrong, breaking down.
On the cards
Possibly.
On the losing end of the stick
To be worse off while the other party to a transaction becomes correspondingly better off
On the pulse
To build upon a person's own experience.
On the rims
Verging on bankruptcy.
Once removed from a Bozzill
Bad-tempered and restless.
One nail drives out another
Two people performing the same service cannot co exist; one danger or trouble dispels another.
One/single track mind
One that cannot be diverted
Open sesame
A necessary preliminary to action.
Open the ball
Make a formal start; begin a quarrel

Open the pack
Tell the news.
Open your budget
Speak your mind.
Open your poke and sell your wares
Open your mouth and tell your thoughts, your opinion.
(To be an) Ostrich
One who wilfully avoids facing the facts, reality.
Ostrich effect
Avoiding risky situations by pretending that they don't even exist.
Our marriage is on the rocks
Marriage is going through a difficult phase.
Out of the blue
Totally unexpected
Out of the picture
Irrelevant; excluded; uninformed.
Owl
A night person
(An) Ox
Refers to a big and strong man.

P,Q

Packet-boys
Small clouds driven before the wind.

Painful lesson in life
A painful situation in life which teaches one a lesson.

Paint a black/bleak/gloomy
Picture/prospect Describe in the worst terms.

Paint him in his proper colours
Describe him accurately and without flattery.

Paint him with his warts/warts and all
Spare no detail

Paint in bright colours
Describe favourably, optimistically.

Palmy days
Triumphant and good times.

Paper candidate
A candidate who puts no effort into his campaign and is just a name on the ballot.

Paper-hearted
To be feeble.

Paper-thin
To be inadequate.

Parthian shot
Parting and telling remark, glance etc.

Pass the hat
Collect money for a particular cause

Pass with flying powers
To be very successful in a test or contest

Patch up (something)
Repair

Patched up
Bodged, hurriedly constructed—'a patched up affair'

Pay the ferryman
To pay the final price.

Peachy
To be pretty.

Pedlar's/tinker's news
Old news.

Peggy with her lantern
Elusive person.

Penelopize
To procrastinate.

Penny soul never comes to twopence
Of natural limitations.

Pick/take up the thread(s)
Resume something previously interrupted.

Pied Piper
Someone who exercises an uncanny charm to lure people away from where they should be.

(A) Pig
To eat a lot; be very dirty in matters of hygiene.

Piggyback
Assist, subsidise.

Piggyback heart
A second heart introduced by surgery into a patient whose own heart needs supplementing.

Piggyback rail/car
Flat railway wagon for carrying trucks or containers.

Pincer movement
Twofold attack on enemy position, cutting them off from each side.

Pinchbeck
False, spurious.

Pivotal
Playing an essential part

Planet-struck
Extremely shocked.

Plans are still a little hazy
Plans are still undecided.

Plateau effect
Occurs when a previously effective measure stops working.

(A) Platform
An area from where one's views can be shared.

Play one tune and dance another
Say one thing and do another.

Play patty-cake with...
Either direct or submit to a relationship with someone.

Please the pigs
If all is well; if the fates or circumstances permit.

Plug gaps
Fill in gaps.

Podunk
Something of little significance.

Point of no return
Reaching a position wherein it is difficult to go back from.

Poison pill

A provision in an act which defeats its initial purpose.

Polish off

Dispose of.

Polished

Cultured, refined.

Polonian

To be sententious.

Pork barrel legislation or patronage

Acts of government that favor special interest groups.

Position

A take on some issue etc.

Position: One's position on a political issue

A belief is a location.

Pray to God but keep hammering

Combine faith with action.

Preach to the converted

To say something to those who already believe in it

Press/push the button

Take a decisive initial step; perform a necessary action to produce the desired result

Procrustean bed

Accepted standard which must be adhered to.

Procrustean

Imposing a brutal uniformity.

Promethean man

One who arrogates the creative function of God in order to give men independence and technical skills.

Pull a dead lion's beard off

Exhibit false valour.

Pull the chocks away

Depart. Be off; time you were going.

Pull the pin

Part company, quit a job

Pull the right string

To do something the correct way.

Pull your freight

Depart soon or suddenly.

Pull/take the chestnuts out of the fire with the cat's paw

Get someone else to do your unpleasant work.

Puppet government

A government manipulated by foreign power.

Push the envelope

Explore, pioneer beyond the point previously reached.

Put a loop in your life

Make a new start.

Put a night on the yarn-winds

To have a boring evening.

Put a ring around that
To be sure of something.
Put every iron in the fire
Try every means.
Put grit in the machine
Interfere.
Put him in a hole
Swindle; defraud someone with whom you should be sharing.
Put in the picture
Inform fully.
Put in your clutch
Go quiet.
Put into the crucible
Renew.
Put on hold
Suspend production
Put one's head in a wolf's mouth
Take an unnecessary risk .
Put out on the shool/shovel
Cast out of doors; disown
Put the irons in the fire
Prepare to do a job.
Put your finger in the dike
Use little means, plus faith and perseverance, to achieve great ends.
Put your hand up
Confess.
Quicksilver
Rapid changes of mood and temperament.

R

Race
A competition.

Rag-bag of Motley
collection of items or people, miscellaneous collection of (usually) incompatibles.

Railroad
Unceremoniously hustle through or out, force peremptorily, convict innocent people summarily.

Rainbow of flavours
A mixture of different flavours.

Raining cats and dogs
Raining heavily; heavy downpour.

Rain-maker
Successful representative of a firm.

Rap over the knuckles
Criticize.

Ratchet up/down
Increase or decrease by small amounts.

Ratchet-mouth
Person who talks a lot.

Read him like a book
Be thoroughly familiar.

Read into
It look into and understand something.

Read on one side of the leaf
To see only one perspective of a situation.

Ready for Blind Charlie's cart
Of something so decrepit that only a blind person would accept it.

Reality is an enemy
Reality is not as good and easy as it is made out to be.

Reams of...
Large quantities of...

Recharge the batteries
Restore impaired faculties and energies by rest and other refreshment.

Red ball
Vehicle officially permitted to travel fast

Red card
Signifies a foul (usually in sports).

Red flag
Signifies danger.

Red shoes syndrome
The compulsion to continue with a dancing career in spite of health and age problems.

Red-line

Discriminate by cutting out or marking out.

Red-line

Push to the limit

Reeking of infidelty

When said about a cheating partner, this doesn't actually mean that there is a literal smell. Instead, it is just apparent that the person is cheating.

Reel in

Bring in; trap.

Rest on one's laurels

To use a reputation for success earned in earlier times as a substitute for current endeavour

Rest on our laurels

Retire whilst being content with one's achievements.

Retread

Retrain people for new jobs.

Reverse ferret

Turning against one's own previous remarks.

Reverse the ratchet

Start moving or working in the other direction.

Ride the hatch

To be censured.

Rider

Something that attaches something new to an existing bill.

Riding coattails

Victories by local or state politicians caused by the popularity of more powerful politicians.

Rise from the ashes

Revive, return to normal after a disaster; find renewal in destruction

Road Hog

Territorially aggressive driver.

Robin Hood's choice

This or nothing.

Robin Hood's miles

Longer than usual.

Robin Hood's pennyworths

Of what is sold cheap because cheaply or dishonestly acquired.

Rock

To be strong.

Rock

Certainty is a solid. (See: drifter, airhead).

Rocked in a stone cradle

Weak in the head.

Rod in pickle for you

A punishment awaiting one.

Rod of iron

Severe discipline.

Roll in dough

To be very rich.

Roll out the red carpet

To treat royally.

Rollercoaster of emotions

When people are on a rollercoaster of emotions, they are simply experiencing lots of ups and downs.

Roman holiday
An occasion at which profit is a by-product of suffering.

Rosetta Stone
A crucial element in the decoding of something/one.

Rough side downwards
Coarse-mannered, angry.

Rough-hewn
Plain, blunt, unpolished, ill-mannered

Roundabout is a turtle shell
A roundabout, like a turtle's shell, is narrow and has little space.

Rug Rat
Infant

Rule out the possibility
To exclude that which cannot happen or that which has been denied.

Run away with
To do something impulsively.

Run like a skeiner
To move very fast.

Run out of gas
Lose impetus, begin to fail, become ineffective.

Run-of-the-mill
To be ordinary.

S

She's quite a catch
Meaning that a person is a good choice.
Sacred cow
Ideal.
Sacrificial lamb
A candidate who is put forward to run for office but who has no chance of winning.
Safety-valve
Harmless outlet for excitement.
Sail close to the wind
To take a considered risk
Salad bowl
A society in which cultural groups retain their unique attributes.
Sandpaper
Refine, generally.
Say that one is about to explode
To reach one's limit of patience; get very angry.
School is a gateway to adulthood
School prepares one for one's life as an adult.
School ma'am(ish)
A conventional woman who is very particular and commands authority.
School your temper
Bring under control.
Scrap-heap Pile of useless metal
Often describing a ruined vehicle.
Scratch the surface of...
Make only a superficial impressio on.
Scream the place down
Report a burglary to the police.
Screw down on:...
Impose restrictions on...
Screw him up
Bring him to the point of concludin a bargain or agreement.
Screw the nut
Pull yourself together.
Screwed up
Highly nervous.
Sea of grief
Very sad
Sealed off
Being impenetrable.
Sealed/closed book
A mystery that cannot be revealed.
Seamless web
Something without a pause.

Search-engine
Computer program for finding words and phrases within a document or database.
Season of change
Change is natural, occurring in phases
Season
Current situation.
Seasoned
Well-tried, experienced
Secreted
Facts hold physical space, and may need to be concealed.
Seduce
To try to make someone to do something wrong by making them an attractive offer of any sort.
See red
To get angry.
See the color of someone's eyes
To see how a person matches expectations or requirements
See what makes the wheels go round
Get familiar with a place's working arrangements.
Seeing pink elephants
Hallucinations caused by alcohol or recreational drugs.
Seize (up)
Refuse to function, fail under stress.
Send a baby on an errand
Invite failure by the way you organise your work.
Send a husband into cornwall without a boat
Cuckold him.
Send a sow to minerva
To teach someone who is more learned and experienced than oneself.
Send her down
Hughie! An appeal for rain or surfing waves.
Sermons in stones
Lessons learnt from nature.

Set a caird, and he'll ride to the devil
None so proud or reckless as those who have risen in the world.
Set high on the wheel
Be very fortunate.
Set him on his feet
Give him a new start.
Set the tortoise to catch the hare
Attempt the impossible.
Set the wheels in motion
To institute appropriate action
Sets the low
Brings on herself the misfortune planned for another.
Seventh heaven
Highest level of bliss.
Shady character
A negative and suspicious person.
Shake the lead out of your pants
Start some action, speed up

Sharpen your pencil
To prepare to work.
She flew like the wind
She ran very fast/at a very high speed.
She followed in her mothers' footsteps
She was just like her mother.
She had returned from the edge of death
She had almost died.
She is bewitching
She is magically attractive.
She is his latest flame
She is his latest lover.
She is my better half
She is a better part of me.
Sheepish
To be embarrassed or shy.
Shift gears
Move from one system of working to another, from one way of thinking to another, from one attitude, policy, method or philosophy to another.
Shift into top/high gear
Begin to work more seriously and efficiently.
Shining example of democracy
A good example of democracy.
Shining example
To be a good model, lesson etc. that can be followed.
Shock-absorber
Mitigating element in a potentially unpleasant or even horrific situation.
Shoed in the cradle and barefoot in the stubble
Prosperous in youth, poor in age.
Short-circuit
Apply or proceed directly instead of through the usual channels.
Short-circuit something
To do something, eliminating various intermediate steps..
Show one's true colours
To disclose one's true colours
Show someone the ropes
To explain how to do a task.
Shrew
A person who complains a lot.
Shrimp
Someone who is small.
Shunt into a siding
Relegate, postpone, treat with less urgency, deliberately ignore.
Shunt something somewhere else
Remove something that is unwanted or in the way.
Shut up like an oyster
To become silent
Shuttle-witted
To be inconstant.
(A) Shylock
To be a heartless money-lender.
Side-slip
Deviate laterally from the previous or planned direction.
Side-track
Divert from proper business; evade the issue.

(A) Silver bullet
A straightforward solution that will have a sure and immediate effect.
Singing the blues
Being sad.
Siren Dangerously
Fascinating woman.
Sit on the safety-valve
Follow policy of repression.
Sketch in
Give a rough outline.
(To) Skid on...
Make a mistake, error of judgement; of prices, fall rapidly.
(A) Skunk
Someone who is disliked.
Sky-pilot
Vicar, spiritual guide, confessor.
Slack-spun
Retarded.
(A) Slate
Scold severely.
Sleck-trough
Prostitute.
Sling ink
Write controversially.
Sling mud
Defame, slander.
Slip the girths
Come to grief
Slippery slope
A small step may lead to a lot of unpredictable big changes.
Sloth
To be very lazy.
Smell of the baby
Not yet have outgrown childish ignorance.
Snail
A slow person.
Snake oil
Fake or unproven medicine.
Snake
To be a traitor, a cunning person
Snowball effect
A situation which starts small but gradually builds up.
So mean he wouldn't give you a shock
If he owned the powerhouse
So unlucky
If I fell backwards I'd break my nose
(A) Soapbox
A platform from where one can give an impromptu speech.
Soft sawder
Flattery.
Solder (up)
Repair.
Somewhere along the line
At some point in a chain of events.
Son of the soil
Man who owes his living to the land.
Sound-barrier
Some serious obstacle or difficulty preventing further progress.

Sour grapes!
Said of someone who, though badly wanting something, when he finds that he cannot have it, denies having desired it in the first place.
Sow dragon's teeth
To invite enmity.
(A) Spanner
Sexually exciting woman.
Span-new, spick and span
Fresh and smart.
Spare tyre
Roll of fat round the middle of a stout person.
Spark-plug
The brightest member in a group; someone who gets things moving; an inspiration.
Speak like an oracle
With authority, but obscurely.
Speak volumes
To speak a lot.
Speaks as though he would creep into your mouth
Ingratiatingly.
Speck of dirt may clog the works of a watch
It needs very little to damage complex operations.
Spell-bound
Captivated.
Spherical cow
Simplified models of real life scientific phenomena.
Sphinx Enigmatic
Mysterious, inscrutable person.
Spicy new outfit
A flavourful new outfit
Spin a fine thread
Do something of advantage; achieve much.
Spin a long yarn
Exaggerate.
Spin a tale
Tell a story, usually a long exaggerated one.
Spin him/her to the length
Exhaust their patience.
Spin it fine
Run it close.
Spin out
Be spent.
Spin out of control
Go beyond set limits; exceed the point where restraints or sanctions are effective; cost more than was allowed for.
Spin street-webs/street-yarn
Idle about the streets, gossiping
Spindle-shanks
Refers to someone having long, thin, tapering legs.
Spins his wheels
Works pointlessly, marks time, is ready for but prevented from action.
Spit for the white horse
Trust to luck.

Spit on his buttons
Proclaim him a coward.
Spit on the same stone
Belong to the same party; have the same ideals, principles.
Splinter group
A minority that secedes from the main body because of disagreements or a shift in policy.
Square one's loom
To punish someone.
Square peg in a round hole
A worker in an unsuitable job.
Squeaking wheel never wears out
Those who complain most last longest.
Stable
To be consistent.
Stand on your own feet/legs
Be independent, self-reliant, manage without help.
Stand with our fingers in our mouths
Helplessly inactive.
Standing on the shoulders of giants
To develop further from what was established previously.
Star chamber
A secretive group within a government that possesses the actual power instead of the government.
Star is in the ascendant
Rising in popularity.
Star is setting
Influence is declines.
Stare like
Bowse Beass Be inquisitive.
Steady rhythm
To be repeated over time is to be fixed
Steam age...
Ancient and out-of-date; old-fashioned
Steam ahead/along
Make strong, vigorous progress.
Steamed up
So angry or passionate as to urge immediate action.
Steam-roller
Crush opposition by weight rather than by reason or skill.
Steam-roller
The epitome of the forces of authority slow, lumbering, insensitive, irresistible, levelling, slow to start, but once started almost impossible to stop.
Steel your heart/yourself against/to do something
Consciously brace or harden yourself to/against...
Steer clear
To move away from.
Stench of failure
The stench of failure is strong, according to the common metaphor, but of course failing doesn't really smell.

Step on the gas
Hurry, increase speed
Step up
Increase.
Stooge
To mislead a candidate.
Stop ticking
Cease to matter; die.
Stop two mouths with one morsel
Use resources doubly economically.
Story
Book ending, solution, character etc. An ideal, idealised one, often romantically happy.
Straight down the line
Without deviation, frills or irrelevancies.
Strait the pin
Concentrate.
Strand Recurring thread or streak in a character
Continuing process, theme, policy etc.
Strange bedfellows
People who are generally not viewed together.
Strength and dignity are her clothing
Dignity matters more to her than fashion.
Stretch on the bed of Procrustes
Ruthlessly fit or accommodate something or someone.
Strike a chord
To bring back a memory.
Strike a false note
To make an error of judgement.
Strike sparks out of...
Elicit something enlightening.
Strike the right chord
To connect; bring out the desired response.
Strike the right note
To do and say what is correct.
Strike while the iron's hot
Seize your opportunity quickly, before it goes.
String together
Link, arrange in sequence.
(To be) Stubborn
To be persistent
Success is a sense of achievement, it is not an illegitimate child!
The saying is used to reinforce the age-old belief that everyone wants to take credit for something that became a success, either by fluke or by conscious effort. On the other hand, no matter how much effort or creativity may have gone into an enterprise, the moment it is considered a failure, no one wants to take responsibility for it, much like an abandoned infant.
Such carpenters such chips
As is the workman such is his work.
Suck dry
Exhaust the resources; extract the last penny.

Suck it all in

Understand as literal what was spoken in exaggeration, or ironically.

Suck the blood of...

Use up someone's resources.

Suck the marrow out of life

To enjoy life to the fullest.

Sugar-tit

Something that gives comfort.

Sun over the yardarm

Time of day when it is acceptable to have lunch.

Swaddling clothes

Restraints on freedom.

Swallow the dictionary

Using long or unusual words.

Swan-song

Final performance.

Swear his ears through a two-inch board

Swear vehemently

Swear his ears through a two-inch board

Swear vehemently and against the evidence.

Sweat the lead out of...

Work to get the trouble out of a situation.

Swept under the carpet

Hidden without resolving.

Swimming in a sea of diamonds

Being very rich

Swinging the lead

Avoid duty by feigning illness or injury.

Sword of Damocles

An ever-present threat.

T

Tail-spin chaos
The state of panic resulting from loss of control.

Taj Mahal
Last point in excellence.

Take a page out of someone's book(s)
To emulate somebody.

Take food out of the mouths of children
Cruelly to deprive the needy

Take someone to the cleaners
To cheat a person financially

Take soundings
See how things are going.

Take the breeks off a Highlander
Do something superfluous and unnecessary

Take the ferry
To die.

Take the heat out of the situation
Allow tempers to cool; pacify.

Take the rag off the bush
Surpass everything or everyone.

Take the rag off the hedge
Surpass, rouse admiration.

Take the rap
To take responsibility for something that has been done wrong by one.

Taken aback
To be taken by surprise.

Taken as
the whole meaning.

Tale in/of a tub
Idle talk, senseless fiction; old wives' tale.

Tangle with
Confront.

Tank up
Drink to capacity, drink heavily; fill up with...

(To) Tantalize
Torment by keeping desirable objects just out of reach.

(To) Tarnish (someone or something)
Spoil something's lustre/someone's reputation by an unworthy act .

Teach your father to get children!
To one giving unnecessary advice.

Teach someone a lesson
Make one learn that he/she has done wrong.

Tear someone apart
Ruthlessly destroy another person's case

Tease out
Elicit by persistently trying.

Teddy bears' picnic
Innocent enjoyment.

Teething troubles
Initial hitches, drawbacks in something new.

Tell a tale
Reveal amazing events, secrets.

Tell tales out of school
To reveal secrets that could cause damage.

Tell the tale
Speak plausibly, speciously; elicit sympathy with hard-luck story.

Tepid speech
A mild speech.

That has been very hard to do
That has been very difficult.

That is a horse of a very different color
That is a different matter altogether

That is cold comfort
Refers to something which appears on the surface to be reassuring, but in reality, it is not

That is the way the cookie crumbles
That is the actual situation

That kindled love in his heart
Something that sparks the feeling of love in one's heart.

That which will not be spun, let it not come between the spindle and the distaff
Do not ask for trouble by putting yourself in the way of it.

That's a different rub of the spindle
A different matter.

That's for the father and no for the son
Of work done with such poor materials it will not last a generation.

That's old Mother Hubbard!
That's incredible!

Thats my mantra!
Belief or philosophy.

The anvil does not fear the hammer
Retort to a threat of violence.

The background
Inconspicuousness.

The best carpenters make the fewest chips!
Commenting that whores seldom have children.

The best o' wabs are rough at the roons
People can be worse than average at the beginning or end of their lives—or in their marginal activities.

The Big Apple
Term used to refer to New York (USA).

The bitter end
Till the very end, be it rough or not.

The black bear of Arden
Object of terror.
The blackest thoughts of men
The darkest and scariest thoughts.
The blues
Referring to sad songs.
The business was about to take flight
The business was about to start.
The carpenter is known by his chips
His work is evidence of a workman's
The clock is ticking
Time is running out
The close the book on something
A terminate an activity
The coast is clear
There are no observer's to one's activity
The cold wind of change
The unpleasant realities a new circumstances.
The daddy of them all!
The biggest, most exceptional, most remarkable.
The damsel of the wood
The silver birch.
The dog and his shadow
One who gives up the substance for the illusion.
The domino effect
A chain reaction.
The end of the bobbin
To be finished.
The end of the chapter
Till death.
The end of the rainbow
Time or place when hopes and dreams come true.
The fairest flower of our garland
Our prize possession.
The farther from stone the better the church
More care is taken with scarce or expensive materials.
The father (and mother) of
Someone or something exceptionally large or severe.
The first thread is not part of the yarn
One word or saying should not be
The golden ball rolls to everyone's feet once in a lifetime
Everyone gets lucky at least once in their life.
The hare and the tortoise
A situation or a pair of characters where the slow and steady one gains the ultimate advantage over a quicker, but over-confident opponent .
The height of one's career
Highest point of one's career.
The height of ten pennyworth of brass
Very small.
The honeymoon is over
Relations which were earlier good are no longer enjoyable.

The light of my life
The person described by this metaphor isn't really providing physical light. He or she is just someone who brings happiness or joy.

The little wimble will let in the great auger
Small beginnings lead to great consequences.

The loan of the oyster catcher to the seagull
The loan never repaid.

The man with the brass knackers
The boss.

The many-headed beast
Many of one thing.

The Midas touch
The talent of a successful businessman; flair for making money.

The milk of human kindness
Genuine natural affection.

The mountain was in labour and produceda mouse
After great expectations, a poor outcome.

The news inflamed her temper
The news made her very angry.

The noise is music to my ears
A sweet and pleasant sound; a good news for the listener.

The nurse is valued till the child is done sucking
A sort of cupboard love, esteemed only while useful.

The nuts and bolts of...
The practicalities, working details of.

The one that got away
Somebody or something that escaped.

The pigeons fountained into the air
The great quantity of pigeons symbolize great happiness, flying off in groups to enlighten various people.

The point of conclusion
The end.

The raven said to the rook 'stand away, black coat!'
Rebuke from one who merits the same.

The road to peace
A journey for peace.

The sea is a hungry dog
The sea swallows anything and anyone that attacks/threatens it.

The shank of the evening/day
The last remaining part

The smith and his penny are both black
The character of a person can be inferred from the state of his property or relations.

The smith has always a spark in his throat
Thirsty.

The squeaky wheel gets the grease
The more fuss the quicker the response.

The steam that blows the whistle never turns the wheel

While they're talking they're not working; mere talk gets us nowhere.

The swine has run through it

Of a marriage gone wrong.

The thread breaks where it is weakest

The failure of a person or enterprise originates from some flaw or feebleness.

The tow

Make yourself ready for your hopes.

The underdog

The weaker one.

The viper and the file

A case of the biter bit.

The waters of Lethe

oblivion.

The wheel has come full circle

A complete reversal of events has occurred.

The whiter the cow, the surer it is to go to the altar

The richest prizes are taken first.

The wish is father to the thought

We believe what we want to believe.

The witching hour

Midnight, when witches supposedly are active.

Theirs is a perfect match

They are perfect for each other.

There are fairies at the bottom of the garden

Something unusual, inexplicable, marvellous is happening hereabouts.

There were giants in those days

The men of old were better, mightier than modern men.

There's ay a wimple

Something suspicious.

There's a fire in my heart and you fan it

You fulfil the burning desire for love in my heart.

They don't make 'em like that any more

Spoken in admiration of someone practising the old-fashioned virtues; of anything valued in its day but now outmoded.

They fed him with a fire-shovel when he was young

To account for his wide mouth.

They have more tow on their distaffs than they can well spin

More to do than they can manage.

They were "all over the place"

To be always around; annoying

They were kindling a new romance

They were starting off with their romance.

Thick as glue

To be very close to someone or something.

Thick as two Jews on a pay-day
In close collaboration.
Thick spinning
Bad behaviour, generally.
Thin as a witch's tit
Of a bowl given insufficient bias to get near the jack.
Things are going smoothly
Things were going well.
Think/work along/on the same lines
Independently of each other, but both using similar methods and moving towards the same destination, conclusion or solution.
Thinks the sun shines out of his/her arse!
Thinks he/she can do no wrong.
Third rail
An issue which is so controversial, pursuing it or even attempting to address it could end one's political career.
This beats my grandmother
Of something astounding.
This won't buy the baby a new frock
We are achieving nothing like this.
Thread and thrum
The whole of anything; good and bad together; miscellaneous scraps.
Thread way
Through Pervade.
Throw a spanner in the works
Upset the proper working by a deliberate act of sabotage.
Throw muck at...
Slander.
Throw of a loaded die
Act of deceit
Throw on the scrap-heap
Cast aside after a lifetime's work.
Throw out of gear/into neutral
Stop someone or something from working; suspend
Throw the baby out with the bath-water
Be so intent on getting rid of what you do not want, that you also lose what you do want.
Thrum-head
Fool.
Thrummy-thrum
Useless, incapable person.
Thumb-nail sketch Brief
quickly produced, word-portrait.
Tick over
Continue to merely function, to operate at minimum capacity; keep going satisfactorily.
Tiger
A positively aggressive person.
Tighter than a witch's cunt often of over
Tightened nuts, bolts or screw tops.
Tight-lipped
To keep confidences; be uncommunicative.
Till Los Angeles river wets its bed
Forever.

Till the cows comes home
For a very long time, perhaps, forever.
Tilt at windmills
To attack unknown problems.
Time is a thief
Time isn't really stealing anything, this metaphor just indicates that time passes quickly and our lives pass us by.
Time is money
Time is a valuable thing, once gone, it never comes back.
Tin god
Absurd object of worship.
To a dot
Precisely.
To a shaving
Precisely.
To a tittle
Exact.
To be poles apart
To have ideas that are very different
To be someone's Achilles' heel
To represent a weakness in an otherwise strong position.
To cage
To enclose.
To disparage
To blame.
To drift apart
To lose contact or to change feelings once held in common
Tolerance is the window to peace
Being tolerant brings peace.
Tom prodger's job
Clumsy workmanship.
Top dog
To be the best person.
Treat like dirt
With disgust; unfeelingly; without respect.
Tried in the furnace
Severely tested.
Trip along
Go lightly and easily—of verse, music etc.
Triton among the minnows
A person who is only recognized well because of the obscurity of all those around him/her.
Trojan
A brave person.
(A) Troll
Stupid person.
Troy was not taken in a day
Used to signify to somebody to be patient.
Truth is Food
Truth is apparently an acquired taste, and one which is still too bitter for most palates, although the bitter foods are often the ones that nourish us most.
Try your skill in galt/gilt first and then in gold
Practise on less valuable materials; also of the unsuitable liaisons of youth.

Tub-thumper
A speaker who complains a lot.

Tunnel vision
Condition of a diseased eye that has lost peripheral vision; blinkered state of mind that recognises only one point of view, and that a limited one.

Turkey
An idiot.

Turkeys voting for Christmas
A suicidal act.

Turn down a leaf
To stop for a while.

Turn over a new leaf
To make a new beginning.

(A) Turntcoat
A person changing sides

Turtle
Refers to a person who moves very slowly.

Twilight
Gloom.

Twine thread could have tied him!
Weakened by coughing.

U

Under her thumb

Under her absolute control, influence.

Under the aegis of...

to be under the leadership of.

Under the veneer of

Superficial pretence for appearance's sake.

Underline

To emphasise.

(To be) Unfold

Reveal

Unhewn

Rough, unpolished.

Unlicked cub

An ill-mannered youngster.

Unpolished

Uncultured, coarse.

Unwind/wind down

Relax after a time of tension, exacting work or overexcitement.

Up and down like a tinker's elbow

Often of something that has worked loose.

(To be) Uptight

To be nervous and cautious.

V

(A) Vegetable

Used to refer to a disabled or paralysed person.

Viper

Contemptible but dangerous and treacherous person.

Voice of a wolf

Refers to voice which is deep and loud

Walk before you run/don't try to run before you can walk
Do not try to make progress too quickly.

Wander about like a lost soul
to roam around aimlessly and dejected.

Wander like a lost Jew
Roam about aimlessly.

Wants it like a baby wants its titty
With an urgent personal need, not so strongly felt by others.

Warm reception
A pleasant welcome.

Warp
Corrupt, cause to grow twisted, perverted, of someone's mind etc.

Warts and all
With the unfavourable features as well as the favourable ones

Wash/wet the head of a new baby
An expression meaning to take a drink to celebrate the birth.

Washing the Ethiop
Working on a useless, pointless and hopeless task.

Way-station
Intermediate stage; unimportant experience through which you (have to) pass.

We are one
When two people are together they consider themselves to be one.

We see not what sits on our shoulder
The obvious is often overlooked.

We were made for each other
We were intended to be with each other.

Weak sister
Feeble, unreliable woman—or man; the failing one in a group, such as a commercial element or branch that is losing money.

Wean from
Cure, distract, rescue from...

Weasel out of
To sneak out from doing something.

Weasel
A person who avoids.

Weathered
Aged.

Weave a tangled web
Get into complicated difficulties, inextricable problems.

Weave a web of sorrow
Sway to and fro like someone uneasy or in trouble.

Weave about
To move in a specific pattern.

(To) Weave
To build or plan or devise.

(To) Wed
To attach.

Wedded to
To be committed to someone or something.

Wedge issue
An issue which turns members of a party against each other.

(To) Weld
Join into a homogeneous unit elements not naturally reconcilable.

We'll just have to go our separate ways
We'll have to break off from each other.

Well-oiled piece of machinery.
To be functioning very satisfactorily

Well-oiled
Complimentary; drunk.

Wet behind the ears
Innocent as a babe; childish, inexperienced—of those who think they are adult but should still, it is implied, be in the care of their mothers.

Wet your whistle
Take a drink.

(To) Whammy
Baneful influence, stunning blow.

What a story!
suggesting that what has been said contains more fiction than fact.

What makes them tick
The secret of a person's motivation, their driving force and the determinant of their actions.

Wheel within a wheel
Someone who acts from concealed or motives.

Wheels down! Prepare to leave
I warn you to leave very soon.

Wheels within wheels
Complex influences at work.

Wheelstring job
Interminable.

When many strike on the anvil they must strike by measure
Where anything is in demand, take turns.

When the knot reaches the comb of the loom, you have to break the thread
When the expected trouble finally arrives, action must be taken.

When you're feelin' blue
When you are feeling low. Blue=low.

Where the rubber meets the road
The lower ranks, grass-roots membership.

Whip and a bell
Something that distracts from comfort.
Whipping boy
Scapegoat.
Whirlwind romance
Romance that is phenomenal and brief
Whistle in the dark
To feign greater confidence than one really has
Whistle-stop
A small, remote place with too few inhabitants to warrant a
White as the driven snow
To be pure white.
White elephant
A very valuable but useless possession.
White glove
Inspection.
Whitestone days
To be remembered with pleasure.
Who breaks a butterfly upon a wheel?
Putting in a great amount of effort for something trivial.
Why do you keep exposing your dull brain?
Why do you keep revealing your stupidity?
Win with a feather and lose with a straw
To be inconstant.
Wind him a pirn
To take revenge.
Wind until a pirn
To enter a difficult position.
Wind up in...
End up in
Wind up
To end.
Wind up
To finish.
Winds of change
Referring to change as the product of forces
Wired up
Nervously excited, ready for action
Wire-drawn
Of extreme or idle subtlety.
Wiry Lean
Sinewy and untiring.
Witch-hunt
A hysterical pursuit of political enemies
With as good a will as ever I came from school
Gladly.
With flying colours
Victorious.
With open arms
To welcome someone cordially.
Withers are unwrung
Unaffected.
Wizard
Computer program enabling the user to perform a complex sequence

of actions by choosing options logically presented on the screen.

Wolf in sheep's clothing

Evil person pretending to be friendly.

(A) Wolf

A negatively aggressive person.

Wooden-headed

Dull-witted. slow mentally.

Words are false idols

Words tend to distract one from reality.

Work like a dog

Hard work.

Work overtime

Work exceptionally hard, fast and effectively.

Work the oracle

Obtain a favourable result by mysterious means.

Worth a Jew's eye

Very valuable.

Would charm the heart of a beggarman's crutch

Of discordant singing or whistling.

Wouldn't give him the hole in a washer for it!

Of an article considered worthless.

Wouldn't say boo to a battledore

Is very timid.

Wrangle for an ass's shadow

Contend about trifles.

Wrapped

In his mother's smock Born lucky,

Wrapped around the axle

Tangled up in minor details; bogged down in fruitless discussions.

Wreathed in

Surrounded by.

Write the book

To be the main authority.

Written all over his face

Obvious.

Y, Z

Years know more than books
Experience provides more than learning.
Yellow card
Signifies a warning.
Yellow-bellied lizard
Someone who is cowardly.
You are the light in my life
You are the sole source of happiness in my life.
You are the sun in my sky
To love someone madly and make that person the most important in one's life.
You can read his mind like an open book
He can be easily understood.
You can't bore an auger hole with a gimlet
Some workers cannot in their nature perform some tasks.
You can't drive a nail of wax
Boys cannot be made to do men's work.
You can't judge a car by its paint job
Don't judge on appearance alone.
You cry before you are hurt
Complain prematurely.
You had better pull your socks up
Get your life together.
You ride as if you went to fetch the midwife
To someone in great haste.
You're a pretty fellow to ride a goose a gallop through a dirty lane!
Refers to a smartly dressed child.
You're looking for maidenheads!
Refers to something unprocurable, or at least very scarce.
Your friendship is the picture to my frame
Having a memorable friendship which is sought to last forever.
Your minnie's milk is not out of your nose yet
You are too young.
Zoom
Burst of energy, zest, drive.

SIMILES

Introduction

A Simile is a figure of speech that directly compares two things through some connective, usually "like," "as," "than," or a verb such as "resembles." A simile differs from a metaphor in that the latter compares two unlike things by saying that the one thing is the other thing.

Following is a list of Similes and their Meanings. Read, understand and learn them as they may be of great help in your day-to-day conversations and in making sentences as well as in writing good English.

A

As alike as two peas in a pod
Identical or nearly same
As a bridegroom
Eager
As active as quicksilver
Active
As afraid as a grasshopper
Scared
As ageless as the sun
Ageless
As agile as a cat
Agile
As agile as a monkey
Agile
As alert as a bird in springtime
Alert
As alike as two peas in a pod
Identical or nearly so
As alert as chamois
Alert
As alone as a leper
Lonely
As alone as Crusoe
Alone
As ambitious as Lady Macbeth
Full of ambition
As American as apple pie
Typical american
As ancient as the stars
Old
As ancient as the sun
Very old
As angry as a wasp
Anrgry
As arid as the sands of Sahara
Barren
As artificial as clockwork
Fake
As artificial as made ice
Artificial
As audacious as the day
Adventurous
As awful as justice
Awful
As awful as thunder
Very bad
As awkward as a cow on ice
Very awkward

B

As bad as a blight
Bad
As bad as the itch
Unbearable
As bald as a billiard ball
Bald
As bald as a coot
Bald
As bald as a coot
Bald
As bald as an egg
Bald
As bald as a coot
Completely bald
As bare as a lion
Bare
As bare as a stone
Bare
As barren as winter rain
Barren
As bashful as a schoolgirl
Shy
As beautiful as a rainbow
Very beautiful
As beautiful as the sunset
Very beautiful, calm
As big as a bus
Very big
As big as an elephant
Very big
As big as a whale
Very big
As big as an elephant
Huge
As big as the ocean
Huge
As bitter as death
Bitter, hard to absorb
As bitter as hemlock
Bitter
As bitter as wormwood
Very bitter
As black as a sweep
Completely black
As black as coal
Completely black
As black as pitch
Completely black

As black as a crow
Extremely black
As black as a raven
Pure black
As black as a sloe
Very black
As black as a starless night
Black
As black as coal
Black
As black as coal
Very black
As black as ebony
Black
As black as ink
Black
As black as jet
Black
As black as Newgate's knocker
Black
As black as sin
Very black
As black as soot
Black
As black as the ace of spades
Black
As black as the earl of hell's waistcoat
Black
As black as thunder
Black
As black as your hat
Black
As blameless as the snow
Innocent
As blank as an empty bottle
Clean, blank
As blind as a bat
Blind
As blind as a bat
Not able to see
As blind as a bat
Blind, unable to see
As blind as a bat
Completely blind
As blind as a beetle
Can't see
As blind as a mole
Blind
As blind as a mole
Blind, can't see
As blind as ignorance
Blind
As blithe as a butterfly
Carefree
As blithe as May
Carefree
As blue as forget me not
Blue
As blue as indigo
Pure blue color
As blunt as a hammer
Blunt

As blut as the back of a knife
Blunt
As blind as a bat
Completely blind
As blind as a mole
Completely blind
As bold as brass
Very bold
As boisterous as stormy sea winds
Very boisterous, chaotic
As bold as a lion
Sassy
As boring as a wet weekend in Wigan
Boring
As boring as watching paint dry
Boring
As boundless as the ocean
Limitless
As bounteous as nature
Rich in beauty
As brainless as a chimpanzee
Dumb
As brave as a lion
Very brave
As brave as a soldier
Very gutsy
As brave as Achilles
Brave
As brief as a dream
Small time
As bright as a button
Very bright
As bright as a new pin
Very bright and shiny
As brief as time
Of small duration
As bright as a button
Bright
As bright as a lark
Bright
As bright as a new penny
Bright
As bright as a new pin
Bright
As bright as a new shilling
Shiny
As bright as day
Very bright
As bright as noon day
Very bright and shiny
As bright as silver
Very bright
As bright as the light
Bright
As bright as the sun
Bright
As brilliant as a mirror
Brilliant
As brilliant as the stars
Brilliant
As brisk as a bailiff
Alert

As brisk as a butterfly
Adroit
As brisk as a flea
Agile
As brittle as glass
Fragile
As broad as heaven's expanse
Broad
As broad as it is long
Broad
As brown as a berry
Brown
As brown as a bun
Brown
As brown as hazelnuts
Brown
As brown as Mahogany
Brown in colour
As buoyant as wings
Very buoyant, free-flowing
As busy as a beaver
Very busy
As busy as a bee
Very busy
As busy as a cat on a hot tin roof
Very busy
As busy as a bee
Busy
As busy as a bee
Very busy
As busy as a cat on a hot tin roof
Very busy
As busy as a nailer
Hard worker, busy
As busy as a one-armed paper hanger
Occupied
As busy as a one-legged arse kicker
Pre-occupied
As busy as an ant
Busy at work

C

As calm as a cat
Calm, cool
As calm as a millpond
Very calm and still
As calm as a summer sea
Very calm
As calm as death
Calm
As calm as glass
Calm
As careless as the wind
Carefree
As cautious as a fox
Watchful
As cautious as a Scot
Alert
As camp as a row of tents
Camp
As candid as mirrors
Very candid, truthful
As clean as a whistle
Very clean
As clear as crystal
Very clear
As clear as mud
Not at all clear
As cold as ice
Very cold
As common as dirt
Very common, rude, vulgar
As certain as Christmas
Sure
As certain as the rising of the morning sun
Sure to happen
As changeable as the moon
Variable
As changeable as the weather
Variable
As chaste as a lily
Pure
As chaste as Minerva
Chaste
As cheap as dirt
Cheap
As cheap as lies
Cheap

As cheeky as a young bantam cock
Cheeky
As cheerful as a lark
Happy
As cheerful as the birds
Cheerful
As cheerful as the day is long
Happy
As cheerless as the grave
Sad
As cheery as a sunbeam
Cheerful
As chill as death
Cold
As chilly as a tomb
Chilly
As chubby as a cherub
Chubby
As clammy as death
Clammy
As clean as a Dutch oven
Neat
As clean as a hound's tooth
Very clean
As clean as a new pin
Tidy
As clean as a whistle
Clean
As clear as a bell
Clear
As clear as crystal
Clean, transparent

As clear as day
Clear
As clear as daylight
Flawless
As clear as mud
(ironical) very dirty
As clear as noonday
Unblemished
As clear as rock water
Pure
As clear as said of tones
Clear
As clever as paint
Clever
As clumsy as a bear
Clumsy
As coarse as fustian
Rough
As coarse as hemp
Stiff
As cold as a corpse
Cold
As cold as a dog's nose
Cold
As cold as a fish
(unemotional)
As cold as a frog
Cold
As cold as a stone
Cold, emotionless
As cold as a well digger's arse
Cold

As cold as a witch's tit
Cold
As cold as any stone
Cold/Emotionless
As cold as blue blazes
Cold
As cold as charity
Emotionless
As cold as ice
Very cold
As cold as marble
Cold
As common as dirt
Easy to find
As common as muck
Common
As common as pins
Common
As common as poverty
Common
As complacent as a cat
Satisfied
As confident as Hercules
Self-assured
As confident as justice
Confident
As conscientious as a dog
Careful
As consoling as night
Soothing
As contagious as a yawn
Infectious
As contrary as black and white
Contrasting
As contrary as light and darkness
Contrary
As convincing as the multiplication table
Persuasive
As cool as a cucumber
Calm and cool-headed
As costly as an election
Expensive
As countless as hairs
Limitless
As countless as the desert sands
Countless
As countless as the stars
Uncountable
As cowardly as a wild duck
Scared
As cozy as the nest of a bird
Comfortable
As crafty as a fox
Clever, crafty
As crazy as a loon
Lunatic
As credulous as a child
Credulous
As crisp as new bank notes
Crisp
As crooked as a corkscrew
Bent

As crooked as a dog's hind leg
Crooked, bent
As cross as two sticks
Cross
As cruel as Media
Unkind
As cruel as winter
Cruel
As cunning as a fox
Sly
As cunning as a monkey
Crafty
As curious as fish.
Keen
As cute as a baby
Very cute
As cute as a bug's ear
Adorable
As cute as a button
Cute, adorable
As cute as a button
Cute
As cute as a cup cake
Cute

D

As daft as a brush
Daft
As damp as the salty blue ocean
Wet
As dangerous as machine guns
Threatening
As dark as a dungeon
Dark
As dark as midnight
Dark
As dark as pitch
Dark, black
As dead as a doornail
Dead
As dead as the dodo
Dead, extinct
As dead as a dodo
Extinct
As dead as a door nail
Dead
As dead as a doornail
Dead beyonad doubt
As dead as a herring
Deceased
As dead as mutton
Lifeless
As dead as the Roman Empire
With no life
As dead as wood
Dead
As deaf as a beetle
Deaf
As deaf as a post
Completely deaf
As deaf as the billows
Can't hear
As deceitful as the devil
Deceiving
As deceptive as the mirage of the desert
Deceptive
As deep as a draw well
Very deep
As deep as a well
Deep
As deep as despair
Of great depth
As deep as hell
Unfathomable

As deep as the sea
Very deep
As dejected as a wet hen
Gloomy
As delicate as a flower
Fragile
As delicious as a dream
Desirable
As delicious as forbidden fruit
Tempting
As dense as a brick
Very dense
As desolate as a tomb
Isolated
As devoted as a faithful dog
Sincere
As devoted as a mother
Devoted
As different as chalk from cheese
Very different
As different as chalk from cheese
Opposite
As difficult as a beginning
Tough
As difficult as a Greek puzzle
Difficult
As difficult as nailing jelly to a tree
Hard
As dirty as a hog
Dirty
As dirty as a pig
Dirty
As disappointing as wet gunpowder
Disappointing
As dismal as a hearse
Sad
As distant as the horizon
Far
As dizzy as a goose
Dizzy
As docile as a lamb
Innocent
As dreadful as a gathering storm
Dangerous
As dreary as an Asian steppe
Boring
As dreary as an empty house
Dull
To drink like a fish
To drink a lot
As drunk as a beggar
Drunk
As drunk as a fiddler
Drunk
As drunk as a fish
Out of his senses
As drunk as a lord
Extremely intoxicated
As drunk as a skunk
Drunk
As drunk as a top
Drunk
As drunk as fiddler
Very drunk

As drunk as a lord
Completely drunk
As dry as a biscuit
Dry
As dry as a bone
Extremely dry
As dry as a bone
Dry
As dry as a mummy
Dry
As dry as a pommy's bath towel
Dry
As dry as a stick
Dry
As dry as dust
Dry
As dull as dishwater
Very dull
As dull as ditch water
Unpleasant
As dull as lead
Dull
As dumb as a box of rocks
Dumb
As dumb as a mouse
Stupid
As dumb as a statue
Dumb
As dumb as any oyster
Dumb
As dumb as stone
Dumb

E

As easy as apple-pie
Very easy
To eat like a bird
To eat very little
To eat like a horse
To eat a lot
As easy as ABC
Simple
As easy as falling off a log
Easy
As easy as lying
Simple
As easy as pie
Very easy
As easy as shelling peas
Simple
As easy as taking candy from a baby
Simple
As easy as winking
Simple
As elastic as a caterpillar
Flexible
As eloquent as Cicero
Fluent
As elusive as quicksilver
Elusive
As empty as an idiot's mind
Blank
As empty as space
Empty
As enticing as a riddle
Attractive
As essential as the dew
Needed
As expensive as glory
Pricy

F

As fabulous as Aladdin's ring
Amazing
As faint as the hum of distant bees
Faint
As fair as a rose
Fair
As fair as Eve in paradise
Flawless
As fair as the morn
Fair
As fair as truth
Right
As faithful as the dog
Faithful
As faithful as the sun
Dependable
As faithless as fair weather
Faithless
As false as dice
Untrue
As familiar as a popular song
Known by heart
As familiar as an oath
Known

As far apart as the poles
Opposites
As far as the eye can see
Distant
As far as the poles asunder
Distant
As fast as a deer
Quick
As fast as a hare
Rapid
As fast as a horse
Very fast, speedy
As fast as a racecar
Very fast, speedy
As fast as a storm
Quick
As fast as an eagle
Quick
As fast as greased lightening
Speedy
As fast as light
Quick
As fat as a distillery pig
Fat

As fat as a hippo
Very fat
As fat as a pig
Fat
As fat as a porpoise
Fat
As fat as a quail
Fat
As fat as a sheep's tail
Weighty
As fat as a whale
Fat
As fat as butter
Fat
As feeble as a child
Weak
As fickle as friends
Changing
As fickle as the sea
Fickle
As fickle as the weather
Fickle
As fidgety as an old maid
Fidgety
As fierce as a famished wolf
Angry
As fierce as a lion
Fierce
As fierce as a tiger
Fierce
As fierce as wolves
Stern
As fine as frog's hair
Fine
As firm as a rock
Firm
As firm as adamant
Rigid
As firm as faith
Firm
As firm as rocky mountains
Firm
As firm as steel
Firm
Fit as a fiddle
Very healthy
As fit as a butcher's dog
Fit
As fit as a fiddle
Fit
As fixed as fate
Unchangeable
As fixed as the laws of the Medes and the Persians
Fixed
As flabby as a sponge
Flabby
As flat as a board
Flat
As flat as a pancake
Completely flat

As flat as a flounder
Flat
As flat as a pancake
Flat
As flat as the fens of Holland
Flat
As flimsy as gauze
Thin
As flimsy as gossamer
Fragile
As foolish as a calf
Silly
As foul as a sty
Unpleasant
As foul as slander
Foul
As frail as a lily
Infirm
As frail as flowers
Fragile
As frail as glass
Weak
As free as a bird
Free
As free as a breeze
Free
As free as a daisy
Free
As free as a fly
Free
As free as the air
Free
As free as thought
Free
As fresh as a daisy
Fresh
As fresh as a mountain stream
Fresh
As fresh as dew
Fresh
As fresh as paint
Fresh
As fresh as a daisy
Very fresh
As fresh as rose
Fresh
As fresh as sea breeze
Fresh
As friendless as an alarm clock
Lonely
As friendly as a puppy
Playful
As frightened as Macbeth before the ghost of Banquo
Scared
As frigid as an iceberg
Frigid
As frisky as a kitten
Frisky
As frisky as a lamb
Energetic

As frisky as a two year old
Excited
As frisky as colts
Frisky
As frizzled as a lawyer's wig
Frizzled
As fruitful as Egypt
Useful
As full as a fat lady's sock
Full
As full as an Alabama tick
Full
As full as an egg is of meat
Done
As funny as a balloon
Very funny, clown like
As funny as a circus
Amusing

G

As game as a fighting cock
In good spirits
As garrulous as a magpie
Talkative
As garrulous as an old maid
Chatty
As gaudy as a butterfly
Gaudy
As gaudy as a peacock
Gaudy
As gay as a bullfinch
Happy
As gay as a lark
Happy
As gay as the spring
Happy
As generous as a dream
Generous
As generous as a lord
Generous
As genial as sunshine
Genial
As gentle as a dove
Gentle
As gentle as a fawn
Gentle
As gentle as a lamb
Innocent
As gentle as falling dew
Calm, tender
As gentle as sleep
Gentle
As gentle as turtle dove
Tender
As glad as a blooming tree
Happu
As glad as a fly
Happy
As glib as glass
Glib
As gloomy as night
Gloomy
As glorious as the sun
Glorious
As glossy as a mole
Glossy
As glossy as the finest silk
Shiny

As glum as an oyster
Glum
As glum as mud
Glum
As gluttonous as curiosity
Gluttonous
As good as a play
Good, of fine quality
As good as it gets
Very good
As good as new
Good
As good as your word
Great
As good as gold
Very good and obedient
As gorgeous as a Sultan
Gorgeous
As gorgeous as the heavens
Marvellous
As graceful as a fawn
Graceful
As graceful as a swan
Graceful
As gracious as a duchess
Giving
As gracious as the morn
Gracious
As grand as a Greek statue
Grand
As grand as a victory
Victorious
As grand as the world
Vast
As grasping as a miser
Grasping
As grave as a judge
Grave
As great as a lord
Great, powerful
As greedy as a cormorant
Greedy
As greedy as a dog
Greedy
As greedy as a hog
Greedy
As greedy as a pig
Greedy
As greedy as a wolf
Greedy
As grey as smoke
Shady
As grey as time
Grey
As grim as death
Sad
As grim as hell
Grim
As gruff as a bear
Gruff

H

As haggard as specters
Fatigues
As hairless as an egg
Hairless
As hairy as a gorilla
Hairy
As hairy as a mastodon
Hairy
As hairy as a spider
Hairy
As hairy as an ape
Very hairy
As handsome as paint
Handsome
As happy as a child
Happy
As happy as a clown
Happy
As happy as a dog with two tails
Happy
As happy as a king
Happy
As happy as a lord
Glad
As happy as a lark
Very happy
As happy as a pig in shit
Merry
As happy as a rat with a gold tooth
Very happy
As happy as a sandboy
Happy
As happy as Larry
Very happy
As happy as the day is long
Happy
As hard as a rock
Hard
As hard as a stone
Hard, thick
As hard as flint
Hard
As hard as nails
Very tough in character
As hard as granite
Hard
As hard as horn
Hard

As hard as iron
Hard
As hard as marble
Solid
As hard as nails
Hard, difficult
As hard as steel
Hard
As harmless as a babe
Harmless
As harmless as a dove
Of no danger
As harsh as a grating wheel
Harsh
As harsh as truth
Tough
As hasty as a fire
Quick
As hateful as death
Hateful
As haughty as a devil
Arrogant
As healthy as a May morning
Good
As hearty as an oak
Hearty
As heavy as a bag of sand
Heavy
As heavy as an elephant
Heavy
As heavy as lead
Heavy
As heavy as sand
Weighty
As helpless as a babe
Helpless
As helpless as a baby
Helpless
As hideous as the witch of Endor
Ugly
As high as a kite
Very high
As high as heaven
Distant
As high as the stars
High
As hoarse as a crow
Hoarse voice
As hollow as a drum
Hollow
As honest as a mirror
Truthful
As honest as the day is long
Honest
As hopeful as the break of day
Full of hope
As horny as a camel's knee
Horny
As horrid as a murderer's dream
Horrid
As hot as a fire cracker
Extremely hot
As hot as a furnace
Hot

As hot as hell
Very hot
As hot as an over
Very hot
As hot as blue blazes
Hot
As hot as fire
Hot
As hot as molten lead
Hot
As hot as pepper
Hot
As hueless as a ghost
Colorless
As huge as high Olympus
Great
As humble as a worm
Humble
As humble as Uriah Heep
Kind
As humorous as wind
Humorous
As hungry as a bear
Starving
As hungry as a church's mouse
Starving
As hungry as a bear
Very hungry
As hungry as a wolf
Very hungry
As hungry as a hawk
Hungry
As hungry as a horse
Hungry
As hungry as a hunter
Hungry
As hungry as a wolf
Famished
As hungry as the grave
Hungry
As hushed as midnight.
Silent

I

As idle as a Lazzarone
Lazy
As idle as air
Indolent
As ignorant as a child
Ignorant
As illimitable as the boundless sea
Limitless
As illusive as a dream
Illusive, not real
As imitative as a monkey
Uninspired
As immaculate as an angel
Perfect
As immense as the sea
Bountiful
As immortal as the stars
Eternal
As immutable as the laws of the Medes and the Persians
Absolute
As impatient as a lover
Impatient
As imperishable as eternity
Eternal
As impetuous as a poet
Impetuous
As innocent as a lamb
Innocent, not worldly-wise
As inconstant as the moon
Varied; inconsistent
As inconstant as the waves
Variable
As indolent as an old bachelor
Indolent
As industrious as a beaver
Organized
As inevitable as death
Unavoidable
As inexhaustible as the deep sea
Inexhaustible
As inexorable as a grave
Inexorable
As inflexible as a granite rock
Not flexible
As innocent as a dove
Innocent
As innocent as a lamb
Innocent
As invisible as the air
Not there
As Irish as Paddy's pig
Irish

J

As jealous as a cat
Envious
As jealous as a Spaniard
Jealous
As jolly as a sandboy
Jolly
As jolly as a shoe brush
Happy
As joyful as a fly
Fun
As joyous as the laughter of a child
Joyous
As jubilant as old sleigh bells
Jubilant

As keen as a razor
Curious
As keen as hunger
Curious
As keen as mustard
Keen, curious
As killing as a plague
Killing

As kind as consent
Kind
As kind as jesus
Very kind, noble
As knowing as the stars
Knowledgeable

L

As languid as a love-sick maid
Lethargic
As large as life
Huge; large; limitless
As lasting as the pyramids
Ever lasting
As lavish as the moon
Extravagant
As lawful as eating
Legal
As lawless as the stormy wind
Senseless
As lax as cut string
Lax
As lazy as a lobster
Lazy
As lazy as a pig
Lazy
As lazy as a ship in the doldrums
Lazy
As lazy as a toad
Lazy
As lean as a lath
Thin
As lean as a skeleton
Lean
As lean as Sancho's ass
Slender
To leak like a sieve
Full of holes
As lenient as soft opiates to the mind
Linient
As level as a pond
Balanced
As liberal as the sun
Independent
As lifeless as the grave
Lifeless
As light as a feather
Weightless
As light as air
Very light
As light as a cork
Light
As light as a feather
Weightless
As light as air
Weightless, lightweight
As light as down
Light
As light as thistle down
Light

As like as two beans
Identical
As like as two drops of water
Identical
As like as two herring
Same
As like as two peas
Same
Like a cat on a hot tin roof
Jumpy, nervous
Like the wind
Quickly, at a high speed
Like two clappers
Very rapidly
Like a newly hatched chick
Brand new, fresh
Like a soldier on a mission
Focused
Like a ton of bricks
Very heavy
As lithe as a panther
Agile
As lithe as a tiger
Supple
As little as a squirrel
Tiny
As little as Tom Thumb
Little
As lively as a cricket
Cheerful
As loathsome as a toad
Hateful
As lonely as a deserted ship
Lonely
As lonely as the Arctic Sea
Alone
As long as a month of Sundays
Lengthy
As long as my arm
Long
As loose as a goose
Loose
As loose as a rope of sand
'Loose' here means 'incoherent' as of a person's speech
As loquacious as Polonius
Talkative
As loud as a horn
Loud
As loud as a lion
Loud
As loud as thunder
Incredibly loud
As lovely as love
Very lovely
As lovely as the violet
Lovely
As lovely as Venus
Lovely
As low as the grave
Low
As lowly as a slave
Lowly
As lowly as a worm
Low
As loyal as an apostle
Loyal

M

As mad as a bear with a sore head
Mad
As mad as a hornet
Mad
As mad as a March hare
Crazy
As mad as a wet hen
Very mad
As mad as a hatter
Completely crazy
As mad as a hornet
Very angry
As mad as the march hare
Very mad, crazy
As magnanimous as Agamemnon
Magnanimous
As malicious as Satan
Malicious
As many chins as a Chinese phone book
Abundant
As mean as a miser
Mean
As meek as a dove
Meek
As meek as a lamb
Meek
As meek as a mouse
Meek
Memory like a sieve
To have a poor memory, to have difficulty remembering things
As merciless as ambition
Thankless
As merciless as Othello
Merciless
As merciless as the grave
Unsparing
As merry as a cricket
Happy
As merry as a lark
Glad
As merry as spring
Happy
As mighty as a king
Mighty
As mild as a dove
Mild
As mild as milk
Balanced

As mild as moonlight
Mild
Mind like a sieve
To have a poor memory, to have difficulty remembering things
As mischievous as a kitten
Naughty, troublesome
As mischievous as a monkey
Naughty
As miserable as sin
Miserable
As mobile as humanity
Mobile
As modest as a dove
Modest
As modest as a maiden
Modest
As modest as a primrose
Humble
As monotonous as the sea
Routine
As motionless as a corpse
Still
As mournful as the grave
Sad
As much use as a yard of pump water
A lot
As muddy as sheep dogs
Dirty
As mum as an oyster
Shut
As mute as a fish
Silent
As mute as mice
Silent, mute
As mute as the grave
Mute
As mute as the tomb
Quick
As mysterious as a sphinx
Mysterious, inscrutable
As mysterious as an echo
Mysterious
As mysterious as dove
Mysterious

N

As naked as a baby
Naked, exposed
As naked as a jaybird
Exposed
As naked as a peeled apple
Naked
As naked as night
Naked
As natural as life
Natural
As near as dammit
Close
As nearsighted as a mole
Short sighted
As neat as a nail
Neat
As neat as a new pin
Tidy
As neat as ninepins
Neat
As needful as the sun
Needful
As nervous as a long tailed cat in a room full of rocking chairs
Very anxious
As nervous as a mouse
Nervous
As nervous as a whore in church
Nervous
As new as day
New, Fresh
As nice as ninepence
Pleasant
As nimble as a bee
Agile
As nimble as a squirrel
Nimble
As nimble as lizard
Alert
As nimble as quicksilver
Agile
As noiseless as a shadow
Silent
As noisy as a menagerie
Noisy
As numerous as the sands upon the ocean shore
Numerous
As nutty as a fruitcake
Completely crazy

O

As obedient as a puppet
Obedient
As obedient as the scabbard
Dutiful
As obnoxious as an alligator
Irritating
As obstinate as a mule
Very obstinate, stubborn
As obstinate as a mule
Stubborn
As obstinate as a pig
Obstinate
As old as creation
Ancient
As old as dirt
Very old
As old as methuselah
Ancient
As old as the hills
Ancient
As opaque as the sky
Opaque
As open as a smile
Open
As open as day
Open
As opposite as the poles
Opposite
Out like a light
Asleep or unconscious

P

As pale as death
Very pale or white in the face
As pale as death
Extremely pale
As pale as a ghost
Pale
As passionate as young love
Passionate, fiery, intense
As patient as an ox
Patient
As patient as the hours
Patient
As peaceful as sleep
Harmonious
As persistent as a mosquito
Determined
As piercing as light
Piercing
As pissed as a newt
Pissed
As pissed as a rat
Pissed
As placid as a duck pond
Placid
As plain as a pikestaff
Plain, simple
As plain as day
Plain, nothing interesting
As plain as the nose on your face
Flat
As plain as day
Very clear
As playful as a butterfly
Friendly
As playful as a kitten
Playful
As playful as a puppy
Friendly
As playful as a rabbit
Funny and playful
As playful as a squirrel
Playful
As pleasant as health
Pleasant
As pleased as punch
Very pleased
As plentiful as ants
Abundant

As plentiful as blackberries
Ample
As plump as mastiffs
Plump
As plump as partridge
Plump
As polite as wax
Polite
As poor as a church mouse
Poverty-stricken
As poor as dirt
Poor
As poor as lazarus
Poverty stricken
As populous as an ant hill
Populous
As positive as a scotsman
Optimistic
As powerful as a lion
Strong
As powerful as death
Powerful
As powerless as an infant
Helpless
As pretty as a picture
Very pretty, fine, beautiful
As pretty as paint
Pretty
As progressive as time
Advanced
As proud as a peacock
Extremely proud, arrogant
As proud as Lucifer
Proud
As proud as Punch
Arrogantly proud
As punctilious as a Spaniard
Assiduous
As punctual as a springtime
On time
As pure as snow
Pure and innocent
As pure as the driven snow
Pure and innocent
As pure as a lily
True, spotless
As pure as faith
True
As pure as snow
Pure, virgin
As pure as winter snow
Pure
As purple as the heather
Purple

Q

As quarrelsome as the weasel
Troublesome
As queer as a chocolate orange
Strange
As queer as a nine bob note
Weird
As queer as folk
Queer
As quick as a flash
Quick
As quick as a lamplighter
Sudden
As quick as a lightning
Incredibly quick
As quick as a weasel
Speedy
As quick as thought
Rapid
As quick as a wink
Very quick(ly)
As quick as lightning
Very quick(ly)
As quick as silver
Very quick
As quiet as a church mouse
Very quiet
As quiet as a lamb
Noiseless
As quiet as a mouse
Silent

R

As ragged as Lazarus
Ragged
As rapid as lightning
Sudden
As rare as a blue rose
Rare
As rare as a comet
Hard to find
As rare as hens' teeth
Scarce
As rare as rocking horse shit
Rare
As ravenous as a winter wolf
Ravenous
As real as the stars
Real, true
As rebellious as the sea
Rebellious, put up a fight
As red as a beetroot
Red
As red as a cherry
Red
As red as a clown's nose
Very red
As red as a poppy
Red
As red as a rose
Red
As red as a turkey-cock
Red
As red as blood
Red
As red as crimson
Red
As red as fire
Red, filled with vengeance
As red as scarlet
Red
Red as a beet
Embarrassed
As regal as Juno
Regal
As regular as clockwork
Mundane
As regular as sunrise
Regular
As regular as the clock
Regular

As relentless as fate
Relentless
As remote as a dream
Remote
As resistless as the wind
Resistless
As restless as ambition
Restless
As restless as the sea
Impatient
As rich as a Jew
Rich
As rich as careole
Very wealthy
As rich as Croesus
Rich
As rich as gold
Rich
As right as nails
Right
As right as ninepence
Feel well
As right as rain
To feel well
As ripe as a cherry
Ripe, developed
As rosy as a bride
Blushing
As rotten as dirt
Rotten
As rough as a storm
Rough
As rough as hemp
Rough
As round as a ball
Round
As round as a barrel
Circular
As round as a globe
Round
As round as a sphere
Round
As round as an apple
Round
As round as an orange
Round
As round as the O of Giotto
Round
As rude as a bear
Rude
As rugged as a rhinoceros
Rugged
Run like the wind
Run very quickly
As ruthless as the sea
Ruthless

S

As sacred as a shrine
Sacred
As sad as doom
Melancholic
As sad as night
Sad
As safe as houses
Very safe, secure
As safe as a sardine
Safe
As safe as a tortoise under its shell
Secure
As safe as blackhouse
Secure
As safe as houses
Very safe, haven
As safe as the Bank of England
Secure
As safe as the bank
Safe
As salt as a herring
Salt
As salt as sea sponge
Salty
As salty as brine
Salty
As saucy as the wave
Saucy
As scarce as feathers on a fish
Rare
As secret as thought
Secret
As secure as the grave
Safe
As scarce as hen's teeth
Very, very scarce
As seedy as a raspberry
Seedy
As selfish as a fox
Selfish
As senseless as stones
Illogical
As sensitive as a flower
Delicate
As serious as a doctor
Serious
As serious as an owl
Serious

As shallow as a pan
Shallow
As shameless as a nude statue
Shameless
As shameless as sin
Indecent
As shapeless as an old shoe
Shapeless
As sharp as a razor
Very sharp
As sharp as a lance
Sharp, edgy
As sharp as a needle
Sharp
As sharp as a tack
Sharp
As sharp as a thistle
Sharp
As shiny as a new pin
Shiny
As short as any dream
Short
As short as the life of a wave
Small lived
As shy as a schoolgirl
Shy
As shy as the fawn
Introvert
As shy as the squirrel
Introvert
As sick as a dog
Very sick
As sick as a parrot
Very sick
As sick as a dog
Ill
As sick as a parrot
Ill
As silent as the dead
Completely silent
As silent as the grave
Completely silent
As silent as a stone
Noiseless
As silent as the dead
Extremely silent
As silent as the grave
Mute
As silent as the stars
Quiet
As silent as thought
Noiseless
As silly as a goat
Absurd
As silly as a goose
Very foolish, silly
As silly as a sheep
Silly
As silly as calves
Absurd
As simple as A B C
Easy
As simple as a child
Simple

As sincere as sunlight
Sincere
As skinny as a rake
Slim
Sleep like a baby
Sleeping soundly
As sleek as a mouse
Sleek
To sleep like a log
To sleep soundly.
As sleepless as owls
Sleepless
As sleepy as a koala
Sleepy
As slender as a thread
Slender
As slender as gossamer
Slender
As slippery as an eel
Slippery, evasive, not to be trusted
As slippery as a fish
(a person who is not trustworthy)
As slippery as a serpent
Untrusted
As slippery as ice
Slippery
As slow as a snail
With no speed
As slow as a turtle
Slow-paced
As slow as a wet weekend
Slow
As slow as molasses
Moves very slowly
As slow as molasses in January
Slow
As slow as molasses
Slow
As sly as a fox
Cunning
As sly as a fox
Sly, cunning
As small as a sixpence
Small, tiny
As small as atoms
Tiny
As small as paint
Small
As small as the hairs on a gnat's bollock
Small
As smart as albert einstein
Intelligent
As smart as an owl
Smart
To smoke like a chimney
To smoke a lot.
As smooth as silk
Very smooth
As smooth as a baby's bottom
Smooth
As smooth as butter
Smooth

As smooth as glass
Smooth
As smooth as glass
Free-flowing
As smooth as ice
Smooth
As smooth as oil
Smooth
As smooth as silk
Smooth, fine
As smooth as velvet
Free flowing
As snug as a bug in a rug
Comfortable
As sober as a judge
Sober, sane
As soft as a baby's bottom
Soft
As soft as butter
Soft
As soft as down
Soft
As soft as fur
Soft
As soft as putty
Gentle
As soft as silk
Very soft
As soft as velvet
Soft
As soft as wax
Soft
As soft as wool
Soft
As solid as the ground we stand on
Solid
As solid as a rock
Solid, hard
As solid as bricks
Solid
As solitary as a tomb
Solitary
As soothing as the breath of spring
Soothing
As sound as a bell
Sane
As sour as vinegar
Very sour
As sour as crab
Sour
As sour as lime
Sour
As spacious as the element
Spacious
As speechless as a stone
Quiet
As spineless as a jelly fish
Spineless
As spiteful as a monkey
Spiteful
As spotless as lilies
Flawless
As spotless as snow
Spotless

As stale as old beer
Stale, old
As stately as an oak
Stately
As steadfast as a queen
Steadfast
As steady as a rock
Steady
As steady as the sun
Steady
As stealthy as a cat
Secretive
As stealthy as a rock
Secretive
As stern as a judge
Stern
As sticky as jam
Sticky
As stiff as a board
Completely stiff
As stiff as a board
Stiff, hard to bend
As stiff as a poker
Stiff not giving anything away
As stiff as a ramrod
Rigid
As stiff as a stone
Stiff
As stiff as death
Stiff
As still as a log
Still
As still as a post
Unmoving
As still as a statue
Unmoving
As still as death
Not moving
As still as the grave
Unmoving
As stink as a polecat
Stinky
As stinky as carrion
Stinky
As stolid as a cow
Impassive
As straight as an arrow
Straight
As straight as a candle
Straight
As straight as a die
Straight
As straight as an arrow
Straight
As strange as a vision
Queer
Strong as an ox
Very strong
As strong as a horse
Strong
As strong as a lion
Muscular
As strong as brandy
Resilient

As strong as hercules
Strong
As stubborn as a mule
Obstinate
As stubborn as a mule
Stubborn
As stupid as a donkey
Stupid
As stupid as a log
Stupid
As stupid as a post
Illogical
As stupid as a sloth
Supid
As stupid as an ass
Illogical
As stupid as an oak
Stupid
Sturdy as an oak tree
Very strong
As subtle as a serpent
Subtle
As sudden as a snap
Sudden, unexpected
As sudden as lightning
Rapid
As sulky as a bear
Sulky
As superfluous as a fifth wheel
Superfluous, extra
As superstitious as sailors
Irrational
As supple as a snake
Agile
As sure as a gun
Sure
As sure as death
Certain, unavoidable
As sure as death and taxes
Absolutely certain to happen
As sure as eggs is eggs
Very certain
As sure as fate
Uncertain
As sure as God made little green apples
Certain
As sure as sunrise
Certain
As sure-footed as a goat
Sure, certain
As surly as a bear
Gruff
As suspicious as a cat
Suspicious, not trustful
As sweet as a nut
Sweet
As sweet as a rose
Sweet
As sweet as honey
Sweet
As sweet as pie
Sweet

As sweet as sugar
Very sweet
As swift as a deer
Quick
As swift as a flash
Sudden
As swift as a hare
Sudden
As swift as a hawk
Sudden

As swift as an arrow
Rapid
As swift as an eagle
Quick
As swift as lightning
Swift
As swift as the wind
Swift
As swift as thought
Swift

T

As talkative as a magpie
Talkative
Tall as a tree
Very tall
As tall as a giant
Tall
As tall as a giraffe
Very tall
As tall as a poplar
Tall
As tall as a steeple (mast)
Very tall
As tall as maypole
Very tall
As tame as a chicken
Tame
As tame as a hare
Tame
As tame as a house cat
Tame
As tame as a sheep
Tame
As taut as a fiddle string
Taut
As tedious as a guilty conscience
Mind-numbling
As tenacious as a bull-dog
Stubborn
As tender as a bud
Gentle
As tender as chicken
Soft
As tender as lamb
Tender
As tender as shepherd
Soft
As tender as tears
Gentl
As terrible as hell
Horrible
Thick as a brick
Not very smart
As thick as a brick
Thick
As thick as a cable
Thick
As thick as ants
Thick

As thick as blackberries
Thick
As thick as hail
Thick
As thick as thieves
Thick
As thick as thieves
Close friends
As thick as two short planks
Thick
As thin as a lath
Thin
As thin as a rail
Thin
As thin as a rake
Thin
As thin as a wafer
Thin
As thirsty as a sponge
Thirsty
As thirsty as tantalus
Thirsty
As thoughtless as a lark
Thoughtless
As tidy as a candy shop
Clean
As tight as a drum head
Tight
As tight as a drum
Tight
As tight as a duck's arse
Tight
As tight as Dick's hatband
Tight
As tight as teeth
Tight
As tight as wax
Tight
As timid as a rabbit
Very timid
As timid as a fawn
Timid
As timid as a mouse
Timid
As timid as a rabbit (as a hare)
Timid
As timid as a rabbit
Timid
As tiny as a grain of sand
Small
As tired as a runner after marathon
Exhausted
As tired as tombstones
Exhausted
As tough as leather
Very tough
As tough as nails
Very tough
As tough as old boots
Very tough
As tough as leather
Said of food hard to chew
As tough as leather
Tough

As tough as nails
Very tough, hard
As tough as old boots
Difficult
As trackless as the desert
Trackless
As trackless as the sea
Trackless
As tranquil as the summer sea
Peaceful
As transient as lightning
Transient
As transparent as glass
See through
As treacherous as the memory
Unfaithful
As tricky as a box of monkeys
Tricky, complicated
As tricky as an ape (a monkey)
Tricky
As trivial as a parrot's prate
Intricate
As troublesome as a monkey
Naughty
As true as steel
True
As true as the gospel
True
As truthful as a knight of old
Truthful
As tuneless as a bag of wool
Tuneless

U

As ugly as a bear
Ugly
As ugly as a scarecrow
Ugly
As ugly as a toad
Ugly
As ugly as an ape
Ugly
As ugly as sin
Ugly
As unapproachable as a star
Distant
As unattractive as a gargoyle
Not beautiful
As uncertain as the weather
Uncertain
As unchangeable as the past
Fixed
As unclean as sin
Impure
As uncomplaining as a lamb
Accepting
As uncompromising as justice
Rigid
As unconquerable as chewing gum
Invincible
As uncontrollable as the wave
Out of control
As unfeeling as rocks
Cold
As unhappy as King Lear
Sad
As universal as light
Universal
As universal as seasickness
Universal
As unmerciful as the billows
Thankless
As unprofitable as smoke
Unproductive
As unreal as a dream
Not true
As unstable as the wind
Unstable
As unstable as water
Unstable

As unsteady as the ocean
Unsteady
As unusual as a sailor on horseback
Strange
As upright as a tower
Straight and tall
As useful as a cow
Productive
As useless as a chocolate fireguard
Useless
As useless as a chocolate teapot
Useless

V

As vague as a shadow
Not certain
As vague as futurity
Vague
As vain as a peacock
Futile
As various as the weather
Ever changing
As vast as eternity
Boundless
As venomous as a snake
Poisonous
As vigilant as the stars
Alert, watchful
As vigorous as fire
Vigorous
As violent as steam
Violent, noisy
As virtuous as holy truth
Holy
As voiceless as the tomb
Spineless
As vulgar as money
Indecent

As warm as toast
Warm

As weak as a kitten
Weak, not strong

As weak as gnat's piss
Weak

As welcome as a skunk at a lawn party
Not welcome at all

As well as can be expected
Very well

As white as a ghost
Very pale or white in the face

As white as a sheet
Pure white

As white as snow
Pure white

As wise as Solomon
Very wise

As wise as an owl
Wise, sensible

To work like a dog
To work very hard.

Worked as hard as an Alabama cottonpicker
Very hardworking

Y, Z

As yellow as a crow's foot
Yellow
As yellow as a guinea
Yellow
As yellow as jaundice
Yellow
As yellow as saffron
Yellow

As yielding as wax
Yielding
As young as dawn
Young
As youthful as the month of May
Young
As zigzag as a lightning
Zigzag in shape